Accounting for Corporations: Volume One

by Therese Trainor

**DARNLEY
PUBLISHING
GROUP**

ISBN 978-2-923623-70-2

Printed in Canada

Catalog No. TAAC5

Senior Reviewer: Stanley Mroz
Editor-in-chief: Ernest Smith, Ph.D.
Senior Editor: Joanne Labre
Design and Cover: Saskia Nieuwendijk

Accounting for Corporations

Table of Contents

Accounting for Corporations

Chapter One - The Ownership of a Corporation

The Reason for This Chapter

After completing this chapter you will understand that stockholders own the corporation. Their ownership distinguishes a corporation from the sole proprietorship and partnership type of business. The corporate balance sheet does not have an Owner's' Equity section. Instead it uses Stockholders' Equity, or Shareholders' Equity.

Before we replace the balance sheet's Equity section, we must first understand the nature of a corporation. This chapter examines how a corporation comes into being. It considers the typical corporate structure. We will begin to account for corporations by preparing the journal entries for the issuance of stocks.

What Do You Already Know?

In this section of the chapter we ask you to complete a pre-test. It will get you thinking about what you already know about accounting. It will also ensure you have the required knowledge to understand the contents of this chapter. After completing the pre-test, check your answers against the ones provided.

Question One

Martin Tanner starts up a business on May 31, 2004. The business is organized as a sole proprietorship. He personally invests $14,000 cash and a machine valued at $3,000. Use the spaces provided to show the journal entries needed for the start-up along with the initial balance sheet.

Martin Tanner General Journal

Date	Debit $	Credit $

Date	Debit $	Credit $

Martin Tanner Company
Balance Sheet
As at _____

Assets	Liabilities
	TOTAL
	Owners' Equity
TOTAL	TOTAL

Answer to Question One

Martin Tanner General Journal

Date May 31, 2004	Debit $	Credit $
Cash	$14,000	
Martin Tanner, Capital		$14,000
To record the investment of $14,000 cash to start the business.		

Date May 31, 2004	Debit $	Credit $
Machinery	$3,000	
Martin Tanner, Capital		$3,000
To record the investment of a $3,000 machine to start the business.		

Martin Tanner Company
Balance Sheet
As at May 31, 2004

Assets		Liabilities	
Cash	$14,000		
Machinery	3,000		
		TOTAL	
		Owners' Equity	
		Martin Tanner, Capital	17,000
TOTAL	17,000	**TOTAL**	17,000

Question Two

Pam and Peter decide to form a Partnership. They agree to split the business 30% - 70%, that is, Pam will only own 30% of the business, and Peter will own the remainder. The business starts on March 1, 2004 with an initial total contribution of $30,000 cash from the partners. Record the journal entries and show the balance sheet resulting from the start-up. You may use the spaces provided below:

Pam and Peter Partnership General Journal

Date		Debit	Credit
Explanation:			

Pam And Peter
Balance Sheet
As at March 1, 2004

Assets		Partners' Equity	
TOTAL		TOTAL	

Answer to Question Two

Pam and Peter Partnership General Journal

Date March 1, 2004	Debit	Credit
Cash	$30,000	
Pam, Capital		$9,000
Peter, Capital		$21,000
Explanation: To record the investments of Pam and Peter.		

Computations:

$30,000 x 30% = $ 9,000
$30,000 x 70% = $21,000

Pam And Peter
Balance Sheet
As at March 1, 2004

Assets		Partners' Equity	
Cash	$30,000	Pam, Capital	9,000
		Peter, Capital	21,000
TOTAL	**30,000**	**TOTAL**	**30,000**

How This Chapter Relates to Other Chapters in This Book

Chapter One introduces the corporate form of business. We begin accounting for corporations by examining how shares are issued and recorded. We start with the first account in the Shareholders' Equity section of the balance sheet, the Common Stock account.

The remaining chapters provide an introduction to the other Shareholders' Equity accounts. Specifically, Chapter 2 covers Retained Earnings, Chapter 4 looks at Dividends and Chapter 5 inspects the Statement of Retained Earnings. The other chapters provide you with a chance to review these topics.

What Are the Topics in This Chapter?

In Volumes One and Two of Fundamentals of Accounting we considered the Sole Proprietorship form of business. The last chapter of Volume Three examines Partnerships. This book is only concerned with Corporations. The main difference between Corporations and the other forms of business can be found in the Equity Section of the balance sheet. By examining share issuance we begin the corporate accounting process.

Topics Covered in Chapter One	Level of Importance
What Is a Corporation?	
The Importance of Limited Liability	***
How Is a Corporation Created?	
The Certificate of Incorporation	**
The Corporate Name	**
Authorized Shares	**
Public versus Private Corporations	**
Who Owns the Corporation?	
Issuing Stocks	***
The Natural Progression	**
Rights of Stockholders	
The Right to Vote	***
The Right to Profits	***
The Right to Information	***

Topics Covered in Chapter One	Level of Importance
About the Stock Market	
Trading Shares	***
Market Value	**
Journal Entries	
Starting with Cash	***
Shares for Assets	**
The Balance Sheet	
Market Value versus Book Value	**
Tracking Authorized versus Outstanding Shares	**
Organization Expenses	**

Legend

*　　indicates a low level of importance

**　　indicates a medium level of importance

***　　indicates a high level of importance

What Is a Corporation?

The Importance of Limited Liability

A Corporation is considered by law to be an artificial person. This means a corporation is viewed as a separate legal entity. It can take legal action in it's own name, or have actions taken against it. The corporation enjoys legal rights and has legal responsibilities, just like you and me.

Sole Proprietorships and Partnerships do not share in this legal stature. By law, their owners are responsible for all activities undertaken. Their liability is unlimited - they can lose everything they own. In a corporation the owners do not carry this burden. It is the corporation itself that is responsible.

The owners of a corporation enjoy limited liability. This means they can not be held legally responsible for the activities of the business. This feature is extremely attractive to investors. They can invest their money in a business, but do not have to worry about losing their personal assets should the business get into trouble. The most the owners of a corporation can lose is the money they invest. Their liability is limited to this amount. Understandably, corporations form the largest part of business activity in the economy.

Why should the owners of a corporation not be held liable? Because they do not run the business. In a corporation the owners are usually different from the managers. The owners hire managers to operate the business. If the business does well, the owners receive rewards. If not, all they can lose is their investment.

In Accounting we use the Separate Entity Assumption to account for the business, regardless of its form. Recall, this requires us to keep the personal activities of the owners separate from those of the business. We always use this principle. With corporations, this principle is established in law. We distinguish between them by asking who is liable?

How Is a Corporation Created?

The Certificate of Incorporation

We incorporate a business according to the specific laws of a particular country or state. The Certificate of Incorporation is a legal document containing pertinent information about what the business may or may not do. It is used to govern the activities of the business for both legal and managerial purposes. It states the nature and purpose of the business, along with its corporate name.

The Corporate Name

We must include the corporate title in the Certificate of Incorporation. It is distinguished by the words "corporation", "incorporated" or "limited" in the business name. The meaning is legally specific, unlike company or partnership. Owners of sole proprietorships and partnerships are not legally separate from their businesses.

Corporations are the most expensive type of business to create. Formal legal arrangements must be outlined in the Certificate of Incorporation. Sole proprietorships and partnerships can be created under much less formal circumstances.

Authorized Shares

One of the important legal requirements for a corporation is the formation of share capital. Ownership is determined by distributing stocks or shares, to investors. While it is possible to create a corporation using only one share, it would be highly unusual to do so.

The Certificate of Incorporation will contain the number of authorized shares. This represents the maximum number of shares that may ever be distributed. While it is possible to have this number adjusted, to do so requires legal changes. This can prove to be expensive.

It is unlikely that all the authorized stocks will be distributed during the initial start-up of the business. Since a corporation is an artificial person, it can live forever. Thus, it is expected that owners will come and go, and the number of distributed shares will change. Therefore, the number of authorized shares is not usually the same number as the shares distributed. Remember, the authorized number of shares represents the maximum number of shares that may be distributed.

Public versus Private Corporations

Corporations may be organized as either public or private. We note the distinction in the Certificate of Incorporation. It is determined by whom the stocks will be made available to. Private corporations restrict the offering of their shares to a few individuals. Public corporations make their shares available to the general public. We examine this topic briefly in the Stock Market section, later on. Most corporations begin privately, but as they grow they become public.

Who Owns the Corporation?

Issuing Stocks

Once the Certificate of Incorporation is complete, some of the authorized shares will be distributed. Investors will give up either cash, or some other asset in exchange for these stocks or shares. We call these shares "outstanding" because they have been distributed to shareholders.

Below is a typical example of a stock certificate:

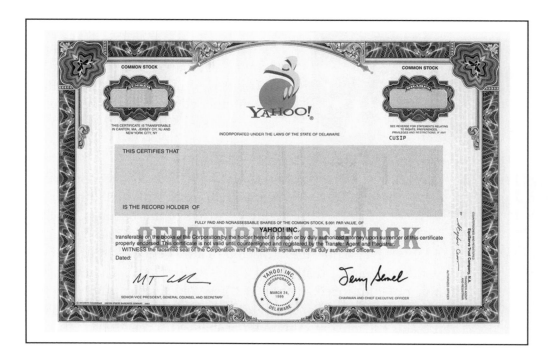

Who gets these stock certificates? How many are issued? It is difficult to answer such questions as each corporation may be different. Instead, let's understand the importance of issuing shares.

The Natural Progression

You have a great idea and decide to start a business. It will be easy and inexpensive to become a sole proprietor. That is why most businesses begin in this form. However, as the sole owner you will have to provide all the money to start it up, and you will bear all the risk if the business fails.

Once your business is operating you will probably need more money to help it grow. You could look for a partner. This may not be complicated if you know someone who is interested. Your partner could provide additional money, but he or she may also want to help you run the business. If it does well, you both share in its success. If not, you are both responsible. That is why your partnership agreement is important.

Continued success of the business will probably create an increased need for money. You could continue to seek out new partners, but they too will probably want to be involved in operating the business. Why? Because they are sharing its liability with you. It will be far easier to attract investors if their liability is limited to the money they invest. At this point it is probably worth the cost of forming a corporation.

Once the corporation is formed, stocks can be issued in exchange for investment. How can you maintain control of your business? By issuing to yourself the greatest number of shares. By giving up stocks in exchange for money you are actually selling pieces of the business. Thus, it is the shareholders who own the business. How much does each stockholder own? That depends on the percentage of shares they buy. Try Exercise One to ensure you understand this idea.

Now You Try It

Exercise One

Alfred Ali has been very successful in operating his sole proprietorship. In order to continue expanding the business, he will need more money. He knows of several potential investors. He incorporates his business. The Certificate of Incorporation authorizes one million shares. Each stock is distributed in exchange for $10. They are sold in the following manner:

Investor	Number of Shares
Alfred Ali	2,100
Suzy Chang	500
Debra Smith	300
Trish Cambo	100

Answer the following questions:

1. How much money did each investor contribute?

2. How many shares are outstanding?

3. What percentage of the business does each shareholder own?

Complete the following table as a guide:

Investor	Number of Shares	x share price ($10) = $ invested	Number bought ÷ outstanding shares = % ownership
Alfred Ali	2,100		
Suzy Chang	500		
Debra Smith	300		
Trish Cambo	100		
TOTAL			

Answers

Answer to Exercise One

Investor	Number of Shares	x share price ($10) = $ invested	Number bought ÷ outstanding shares = % ownership
Alfred Ali	2,100	$21,000	70%
Suzy Chang	500	$ 5,000	17%
Debra Smith	300	$ 3,000	10%
Trish Cambo	100	$ 1,000	3%
TOTAL	3,000 outstanding	$30,000 invested	100% ownership

Clearly Alfred owns the most shares. It follows that he will have the most say in the business. We expand on this idea by examining the rights of stockholders in the next section. You should note that while one million shares are authorized only 3,000 shares are outstanding. It is the outstanding shares that determine the percentage of ownership in the business.

Rights of Stockholders

Once you invest in a corporation, what should you expect? Clearly, your goal is to make money. While corporations may be formed using different kinds and classes of shares, we focus on the most common type. It should not be a surprise that we call these common shares.

Common shareholders expect certain privileges. These are:

1. The right to vote.
2. The right to profits.
3. The right to information about the business.

Common stockholders should not expect to run the business, especially if the corporation is public. We will examine each of the stockholder's rights.

The Right to Vote

While different classes of common stocks may exist, at least one class will have the right to vote. We keep things simple here and assume there is only one class of common stocks. For our purposes, common stockholders have the right to vote.

The voting right attached to each common stock ensures the privilege to participate at the stockholders' meeting. These meetings may be called whenever an important issue needs to be discussed, but they must take place at least once per year.

While stockholders own the business, they do not usually operate it. They decide who will run the corporation. However, they do not go out and actually hire the management team. Instead, stockholders elect a Board of Directors with their votes. This Board oversees the hiring and firing of management. (See next page for a typical organization chart.)

Thus, stockholders elect the members of the Board of Directors. The Board in turn appoints a President. The President hires the Vice-Presidents and employees. If stockholders are unhappy with how the business is run, they can elect new members to the Board of Directors who in turn can change the managers. This important process assures stockholders that management operates the business to improve the wealth of its stockholders.

Organization Structure of a Corporation

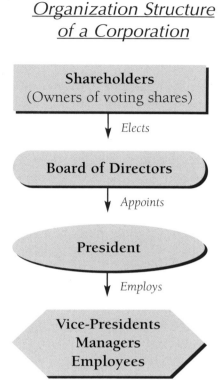

Shareholders
(Owners of voting shares)

Elects

Board of Directors

Appoints

President

Employs

Vice-Presidents
Managers
Employees

The Right to Profits

Investors become shareholders with the goal of making money on their investment. Since it is the shareholders that own the business, they are entitled to any profits from it. However, it does not follow that net income is distributed as cash to shareholders. We examine cash distributions to stockholders in Chapter Two.

Shareholders own net income. Thanks to the limited liability feature they do not have to make up any net loss. We account for shareholders' participation in profits using retained earnings, dividends and the Statement of Retained Earnings. These topics are the subject matter of the remaining chapters in this Volume. For the moment be assured that stockholders have a right to share in the profits of the business.

The Right to Information

How will stockholders know if management is doing a good job? They require information about the business in order to decide how well management is doing. Accounting provides important reports to assist the owners in making such decisions. They should be very familiar to you! The financial statements - the Balance Sheet, Income Statement and Statement of Cash Flows all contribute important information to help stockholders assess the performance of management. Stockholders are entitled to receive these statements at least annually, and usually more often, such as quarterly. The financial reports, along with other pertinent information are placed in an annual report. It is mailed directly to existing shareholders.

About the Stock Market

Trading Shares

Public corporations trade their shares in an organized exchange, known as a stock market. While many stock markets exist geographically, their function is much the same. Stock markets enable investors to easily trade, that is, to buy and sell the shares of corporations.

Millions of investors around the world use stock markets to trade shares. The information contained in the corporation's annual report assists them in making trading decisions. It helps investors determine whether they should buy or sell shares of a corporation. With millions of investors receiving this information it is considered to be public knowledge.

Investors in private corporations also receive information. However, it may not be as formal as an annual report, and it is certainly not considered public knowledge. Because these shares do not trade on large organized exchanges, it is more difficult to buy and sell such shares. Private corporate shareholders must seek out other investors willing to trade these shares. Thus the stock market eliminates the search for investors - they are readily participating in the stock exchange.

Market Value

The stock market also performs another important function. It establishes price. Think back to Exercise One. When Alfred Ali decided to incorporate his business and issue shares, he decides to sell them at $10 each. How did he establish this price? It is incredibly complex to do so.

Professionals in the stock market assist corporations in the effort to determine a stock's price. They earn millions of dollars in fees for doing so. Many stock market professionals are accountants.

It is important to understand that once a stock is sold in the stock market, its price becomes public knowledge. Thus, the stock market reveals the last traded price. Should we wish to buy or sell the same stock, we would expect to trade close to the last price. We refer to the last price as the market price, or value. It represents what the stock is worth, right now. With millions of investors continuously making trades, the market value of a stock constantly changes.

Journal Entries

Starting with Cash

When the corporation starts-up by issuing shares in exchange for cash, two accounts are affected: cash and share capital. The recording and posting process is much the same as for sole proprietorships and partnerships. Just the account names change. Practice accounting for share issuance. Try Exercise Two.

Now You Try It

Exercise Two
Let's revisit Alfred Ali, with some changes.

Alfred Ali has been very successful in operating his sole proprietorship. In order to continue expanding the business, he will need more money. He incorporates his business under the name Computers Incorporated. The Certificate of Incorporation authorizes one million shares. On April 5, 2004 shares are sold for $10 cash to each of the following investors:

Investor	Number of Shares
Suzy Chang	500
Debra Smith	300
Trish Cambo	100

What about Alfred's shares? We will answer this question as part of Exercise Three.

Use the space provided below to prepare the journal entries:

Computers Incorporated General Journal

Date	Debit $	Credit $

Date	Debit $	Credit $

Date	Debit $	Credit $

Answers

Answer to Exercise Two

Computers Incorporated General Journal

Date April 5, 2004	Debit $	Credit $
Cash	$5,000	
Share Capital		$5,000
To record the sale of 500 common shares at $10 each to Suzy Chang.		

Date April 5, 2004	Debit $	Credit $
Cash	$3,000	
Share Capital		$3,000
To record the sale of 300 common shares at $10 each to Debra Smith.		

Date April 5, 2004	Debit $	Credit $
Cash	$1,000	
Share Capital		$1,000
To record the sale of 100 common shares at $10 each to Trish Cambo.		

While it is not improper to record each entry separately, it is far more common that one entry will be made with the details provided in the explanation section, like this:

Date April 5, 2004	Debit $	Credit $
Cash	$9,000	
Share Capital		$9,000
Sold 900 common shares at $10 each to:		
S. Chang 500		
D. Smith 300		
T. Cambo 100		
TOTAL 900		

Notice the share capital account does not contain any specific information regarding who owns the shares. In the partnership and sole proprietorship forms, the equity accounts were always linked with the owner's name. Not so for corporations; separate records are maintained indicating the name, address, etc. of each shareholder and the number of shares owned by each shareholder.

Shares for Assets

When the corporation issues shares in exchange for assets other than cash, we still credit share capital. However, we must account for the specific assets used in the exchange. Instead of debiting cash, we debit the appropriate asset account(s). This process can become complicated because we must first determine the dollar value of the assets. We then calculate the number of shares to be issued in exchange for the assets. Practice issuing shares in exchange for assets other than cash. Try Exercise Three.

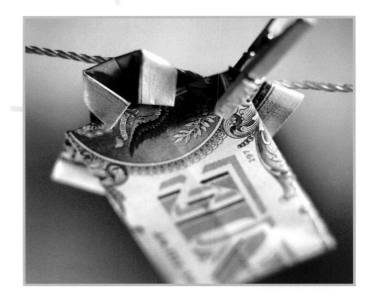

Now You Try It

Exercise Three

Let's continue with Alfred Ali and Computers Incorporated.

Alfred Ali incorporated his business on April 5, 2004. In addition to selling shares for cash, as in Exercise Two, he gave up the assets of the existing business and used them to purchase shares worth $10 each in Computers Incorporated. The balance sheet of Alfred's business, just before incorporation is given below:

Alfred Ali Company
Balance Sheet
As at April 4, 2004

Assets		Liabilities	
Cash	$1,000		
Accounts Receivable	3,000	**Owners' Equity**	
Office Supplies	1,500		
Computer Equipment	15,500	Alfred Ali, Capital	21,000
TOTAL	**21,000**	**TOTAL**	**21,000**

The books of Alfred Ali Company were successfully closed out. We will not examine the journal entries for this process. All the assets were exchanged for shares in the new company, Computers Incorporated at a value of $10 each. Prepare the journal entries for the corporation. You may use the space provided below:

Computers Incorporated General Journal

Date	Debit $	Credit $

Date	Debit $	Credit $

Date	Debit $	Credit $

Date	Debit $	Credit $

Answers

Answer to Exercise Three

Valuing business assets is a complex topic and beyond the scope of this book. We will accept the value of the assets shown on the balance sheet as correct.

Computers Incorporated General Journal

Date April 5, 2004	Debit $	Credit $
Cash	$1,000	
Share Capital		$1,000
To record the sale of 100 common shares to Alfred Ali in exchange for $1,000 cash.		

Computation: $1,000 x 10% = 100 shares

Date April 5, 2004	Debit $	Credit $
Accounts Receivable	$3,000	
Share Capital		$3,000
To record the sale of 300 common shares to Alfred Ali in exchange for $ 3000 Accounts Receivable.		

Computation: $3,000 x 10% = 300 shares

Date April 5, 2004	Debit $	Credit $
Office Supplies	$1,500	
Share Capital		$1,500
To record the sale of 150 common shares to Alfred Ali in exchange for $1,500 worth of Office Supplies.		

Computation: $1,500 x 10% = 150 shares

Date April 5, 2004	Debit $	Credit $
Computer Equipment	$15,500	
Share Capital		$15,500
To record the sale of 1,550 common shares to Alfred Ali in exchange for $15,500 worth of Computer Equipment.		

Computation: $15,500 x 10% = 1,550 shares

Once again, it is not improper to record each entry separately. However, it is a lot of work. Let's use just one entry:

Date April 5, 2004	Debit $	Credit $
Cash	$1,000	
Accounts Receivable	$3,000	
Office Supplies	$1,500	
Computer Equipment	$15,500	
Share Capital		$21,000
Issued 2,100 common shares at $10 each to Alfred Ali for cash and other assets.		

Remember, the share capital account does not contain any specific information regarding who owns the shares. Even though Alfred Ali owns most of the shares now, he could trade them in the future. Doing so changes the ownership structure. Accounting for share capital this way keeps the accounts flexible. Even if ownership changes, the share capital account may not.

The Balance Sheet

Market Value versus Book Value

Do you remember the Cost principle? It requires that we report the value of assets, liabilities and equity on the balance sheet at their historical values. We refer to the account balances on the balance sheet as book values. Thus, the share capital account represents the price shares were sold for in the past. The market value represents how much they are worth today. Hence, we should not expect book and market values to be equal. Obviously, investors would prefer they not be equal. When you buy shares you hope to sell them later for more money!

The share capital account tells us how much money investors have put into the business, through buying shares. We will not account for how much money shareholders may make by selling their shares to other investors. That is the business of the individual shareholder - not the business of the corporation. Remember, we account for transactions related to the business, not for transactions outside it.

Tracking Authorized versus Outstanding Shares

The number of outstanding shares can never exceed the number authorized in the Certificate of Incorporation. Therefore, we must keep track of both numbers. We note them on the balance sheet along with the share capital. Typically, we present that section of the balance sheet as follows:

Example Company
Shareholders' Equity
As at _____

Share Capital

Authorized	10,000,000 common shares	
Outstanding	10,000 shares	$100,000

While we do not expect the number of authorized shares to change, we should anticipate more shares will be issued in the future. Practice additional share issuance. Try Exercise Four.

Now You Try It

Exercise Four

Back to Computers Incorporated! Due to increased demand it sells more shares, for cash, in the following manner:

Date	Name	Number	Price per Share
April 12, 2004	H. Cohen	200	$12
April 23, 2004	W. Manuk	180	$12.50

Use the space provided below to prepare the necessary journal entries:

Computers Incorporated General Journal

Date		Debit $	Credit $

Date	Debit $	Credit $

Answers

Answer to Exercise Four

Date April 12, 2004	Debit $	Credit $
Cash	$2,400	
Share Capital		$2,400
To record the sale of 200 common shares at $12 each to H. Cohen.		

Computation: 200 x $12 = $2,400

Date April 23, 2004	Debit $	Credit $
Cash	$2,250	
Share Capital		$2,250
To record the sale of 180 common shares at $12.50 each to W. Manuk.		

Computation: 180 x $12.50 = $2,250

Notice, the shares need not always be sold for $10! In fact, when there is a lot of demand we expect the price per share to rise. We always record the issuance of shares for the price at which they were sold, regardless of how it changes.

Prepare the balance sheet for a corporation. Try Exercise Five.

Now You Try It

Exercise Five

Post the journal entries from Exercises Two, Three, and Four to the General Ledger for Computers Incorporated. Assume there were no other transactions that month. Prepare the balance sheet dated April 30, 2004. You may use the spaces provided below:

Computers Incorporated General Journal

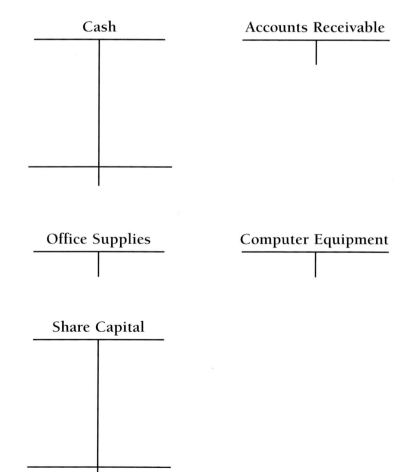

Cash   Accounts Receivable

Office Supplies   Computer Equipment

Share Capital

Computers Incorporated
Balance Sheet
As at _____

Assets		Liabilities	
		Shareholders' Equity	
TOTAL		TOTAL	

Answers

Answer to Exercise Five

Computers Incorporated General Journal

Cash		Accounts Receivable	
5,000		3,000	
3,000			
1,000			
1,000			
2,400			
2,250			
14,650			

Office Supplies		Computer Equipment	
1,500		15,500	

Share Capital

	5,000
	3,000
	1,000
	21,000*
	2,400
	2,250
	34,650

* 1,000 + 3,000 + 1,500 + 15,500 = 21,000

Computers Incorporated
Balance Sheet
As at April 30, 2004

Assets		Liabilities	
Cash	$14,650		
Accounts Receivable	3,000	**Shareholders' Equity**	
Office Supplies	1,500	Share Capital	
Computer Equipment	15,500	Authorized common shares 1,000,000	
		Outstanding shares 3,380**	34,650
TOTAL	**34,650**	**TOTAL**	**34,650**

** 900 + 2,100 + 200 + 180 = 3,380

Organization Expenses

As a final note we remind you that the incorporation process can be costly. Many different types of expenses, such as legal, government and printing may be incurred. Since these costs may be significant, we must account for them. We charge these expenses to the Organization Expense account. While this account may be handled in a variety of ways, we will simply assume all organization costs are expensed at the time of incorporation. Practice this idea. Try Exercise Six:

Now You Try It

Exercise Six:

On June 30, 2004, Some Company decides to incorporate. At that time, the following expenses were incurred:

Expense Type	Amount
Legal fees	$250
Government licenses	$150
Printing of share certificates	$ 50

Prepare the journal entry needed to account for the organization expenses. Assume they are paid immediately. We have provided the general journal space, below:

Some Incorporated General Journal

Date	Debit $	Credit $

Answers

Answer to Exercise Six

Some Incorporated General Journal

Date June 30, 2004	Debit $	Credit $
Organization Expense	$450	
Cash		$450
To record the organization expenses incurred for incorporation: Legal $250 Government $150 Printing $ 50 **TOTAL** **$450**		

What You Have Learned in This Chapter

Chapter One provides a detailed description of the corporate form of business. It highlights the importance of limited liability and why it is attractive to investors. It examines how a corporation comes into being and discusses the role of shareholders as owners. It provides a demonstration of how ownership can change through the trading of shares along with exhibiting the rights of stockholders. A brief introduction to the stock market augments this discussion.

We begin to account for the corporation in this chapter. Journal entries required for share issuance are covered. We introduce the related shareholders' equity account, share capital. The focus in this chapter is on starting up the corporation. Practice with a preliminary balance sheet is also provided.

Important Terms in This Chapter

Annual Reports: contain the financial statements along with other important information. They are mailed once a year to shareholders.

Authorized shares: the maximum number of shares that may ever be distributed.

Book Value: the value of an account balance on the balance sheet.

Certificate of Incorporation: a legal document specifying the activities the business may and may not undertake.

Corporation: the form of business where owners are shareholders. There may be an unlimited number of stockholders. The name includes Corporation, Incorporated or Limited.

Cost principle: the balances on the balance sheet are recorded at their historical cost.

Limited Liability: the owners of a corporation can only lose what they invested. Their liability is limited to this amount.

Market Value: the price of a share, today. Also known as market price.

Organization Expenses: expenses incurred to incorporate the business.

Outstanding Shares: shares that have been distributed in exchange for cash or assets.

Private corporations: restrict the offering of their stocks to a few individuals.

Public corporations: make their shares available to the general public.

Separate Entity Assumption: account for the personal activities of the owners separate from that of the business.

Shares: also called stocks. Certificates issued that represent ownership. Once an investor buys shares in a corporation he/she is deemed to be one of the owners. The number of potential owners is generally unlimited.

Stockholders' Equity: similar function to Owner's Equity but used for the corporate form of business. When shares (stocks) of the firm are issued we record their value as Stockholders' Equity. It represents the investment owners (stockholders) have in the business.

Stocks: see Shares.

Trading: buying or selling stocks of a corporation.

Should You Move on to the Next Chapter?

Now it's time to check and see how comfortable you are with your new knowledge. Perform the Self-Test to verify whether you should move on, or go back and review the information contained in this chapter.

Self-Test for Chapter One

Question One

Why is limited liability an advantage of the corporate form of business? Explain.

_____
_____
_____
_____
_____
_____

Question Two

What is the difference between authorized and outstanding shares?

_____

_____

_____

_____

_____

Question Three

Laura's House of Wares has been experiencing significant growth. Laura Hope started the business, as a sole proprietor, years ago. She alone has worked most of her adult life to ensure the success of the business. Recently, Laura has remarried. On the advice of her accountant, Laura decides to incorporate her business. The Certificate of Incorporation authorizes 10,000 common shares, each with equal voting rights. Each stock is distributed in exchange for $5. They are distributed in the following manner:

Investor	Number of Shares	% Ownership
Frank Hope (husband)	3,000	
Tim Hope (husband's son)	1,000	
Tanya White (daughter)	1,000	
Martha Hope (husband's mother)	2,000	
Laura Hope	3,000	
TOTAL		

Do you think Laura has made a mistake? Hint: calculate the percentage of ownership for each shareholder of the corporation. Use the above table as a guide and provide your explanation in the space below:

_____

_____

_____

_____

_____

Question Four

Nyguen Incorporated has recently issued shares in the following manner:

Date	Name	Number	Price per Share
October 3, 2004	B. Chong	1,200	$7
October 3, 2004	K. Combs	1,800	$7
October 15, 2004	R. Getty	2,200	$7.80

All the investors paid cash, except R. Getty, who exchanged machinery for the common shares. Use the space provided below to prepare the necessary journal entries:

Nyguen Incorporated General Journal

Date		Debit $	Credit $

Computation:

Date		Debit $	Credit $

Computation:

Answers to Self-Test for Chapter One

Answer to Question One

Legally, the owners of Sole Proprietorships and Partnerships are responsible for all activities undertaken. Their liability is unlimited - they can lose everything they own. In a corporation the owners do not have this risk. It is the corporation itself that is responsible.

The owners of a corporation enjoy limited liability. This means they can not be held legally responsible for the activities of the business. This feature is extremely attractive to investors. They can invest their money in a business, but do not have to worry about losing their personal assets if the business gets into trouble. The most that the owners of a corporation can lose is the money they invest. Their liability is limited to this amount.

Answer to Question Two

The Certificate of Incorporation shows the number of authorized shares. This represents the maximum number of shares that may ever be distributed. However, not all the authorized stocks are usually distributed during the initial start-up of the business. This allows the corporation to distribute more shares in the future, as it continues to grow. We refer to distributed shares as outstanding, since they have been issued and are in the hands of shareholders. Therefore the number of authorized shares is not usually the same number as the shares distributed. It is greater.

Answer to Question Three

Investor	Number of Shares	% Ownership
Frank Hope (husband)	*3,000*	*3,000 ÷ 10,000 = 0.30 or 30%*
Tim Hope (husband's son)	*1,000*	*1,000 ÷ 10,000 = 0.10 or 10%*
Tanya White (daughter)	*1,000*	*1,000 ÷ 10,000 = 0.10 or 10%*
Martha Hope (husband's mother)	*2,000*	*2,000 ÷ 10,000 = 0.20 or 20%*
Laura Hope	*3,000*	*3,000 ÷ 10,000 = 0.30 or 30%*
TOTAL (outstanding)	*10,000*	*10,000 ÷ 10,000 = 1 or 1%*

We think Laura has made a big mistake. The recommendation of her accountant to incorporate was probably correct but the way she has distributed the shares is very risky.

Laura has been responsible for the success of the business. However, with each share having an equal voting right Laura has given up control of the business. She and her husband each own 30%. She has given her new husband an equal voice in the business. Even worse, her husband's family has more voting power than her own. They control 30% (husband) + 10% (husband's son) + 20% (husband's mother) = 60% of the voting shares while Laura and her daughter only control 40%. Thus, the wishes of Laura and her daughter could be overruled in the case of a dispute. Although more shares could be issued, Laura may no longer have a say in how they will be distributed. If Laura insists on distributing shares to her family, she should ensure that she alone maintains control by keeping the largest portion for herself.

Answer to Question Four

Date October 3, 2004	Debit $	Credit $
Cash	21,000	
Share Capital		21,000
Sold 3,000 common shares at $7 each to: B. Chong 1,200 K. Combs 1,800 **Total 3,000**		

Computation: 3,000 x $7 = $21,000

Date October 15, 2004	Debit $	Credit $
Machinery	17,160	
Share Capital		17,160
To record the sale of 2,200 common shares at $7.80 each to R. Getty in exchange for machinery.		

Computation: 2,200 x $7.80 = $17,160

Practice Problems for Chapter One

Question One

Kinshasa Martel incorporated a business on May 1, 2004. The Certificate of Incorporation authorized 250,000 common shares. In addition to selling shares for cash, she converted the assets of her sole proprietorship into shares for herself. The balance sheet of Kinshasa's business, just before incorporation is given below:

Kinshasa Martel Company
Balance Sheet
As at April 30, 2004

Assets		Liabilities	
Cash	$ 2,000		
Merchandise Inventory	3,000	**Owners' Equity**	
Office Supplies	1,000		
Office Equipment	20,000	Kinshasa Martel, Capital	26,000
TOTAL	**26,000**	**TOTAL**	**26,000**

The books of Kinshasa Martel Company were successfully closed out. Do not prepare the journal entries for this process. On May 1, 2004, all the assets were exchanged for common shares of the new company, Kinshasa Incorporated at a value of $5.00 for each share. Additional shares were sold for cash in the following manner:

Date	Name	Number	Price per Share
May 10, 2004	R. West	250	$6
May 25, 2004	N. Greene	300	$7

No other transactions occurred during the month of May. Prepare the journal entries and post them to the ledger. Prepare the balance sheet dated May 31, 2004. You may use the spaces provided below:

Kinshasa Incorporated General Journal

Date	Debit $	Credit $

Computation:

Date	Debit $	Credit $

Computation:

Date	Debit $	Credit $

Computation:

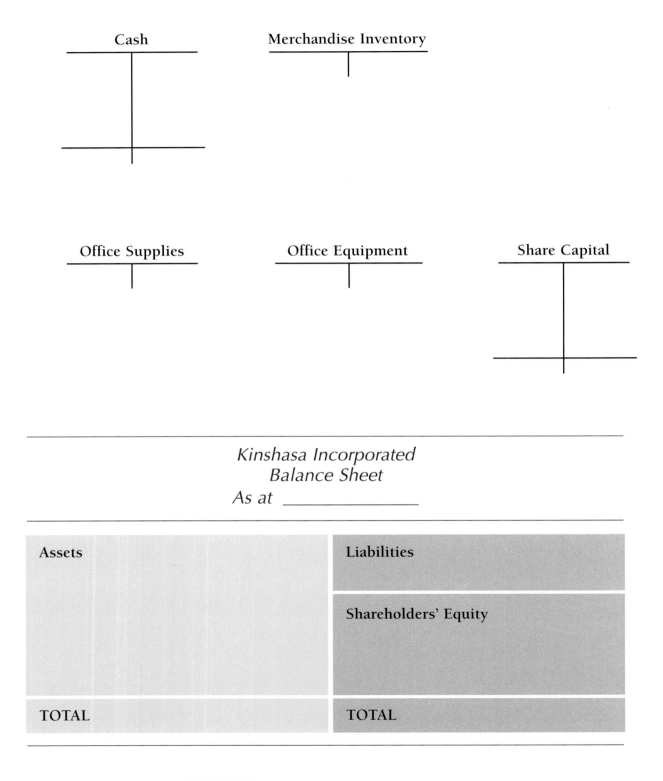

Kinshasa Incorporated General Ledger

Cash

Merchandise Inventory

Office Supplies

Office Equipment

Share Capital

Kinshasa Incorporated
Balance Sheet
As at _____

Assets	Liabilities
	Shareholders' Equity
TOTAL	TOTAL

Question Two

On December 1, 2004 the Alabaster Partners became Alabaster Corporation. At that time, the following expenses were incurred:

Expense Type	Amount
Legal fees	$1,000
Government licenses	$ 200
Printing of share certificates	$ 150

Prepare the journal entry needed to account for the organization expenses. Assume they are paid immediately. Use the general journal space, below:

Alabaster Corporation General Journal

Date		Debit $	Credit $

Solutions to Practice Problems for Chapter One

Solutions to Question One

Kinshasa Incorporated General Journal

Date May 1, 2004	Debit $	Credit $
Cash	2,000	
Merchandise Inventory	3,000	
Office Supplies	1,000	
Office Equipment	20,000	
Share Capital		26,000
Issued 5,200 common shares at $5 each to Kinshasa Martel for cash and other assets.		

Computation: $26,000 ÷ $5 = 5,200 shares

Date May 10, 2004	Debit $	Credit $
Cash	1,500	
Share Capital		1,500
Explanation: Sold 250 common shares at $6 each to R. West.		

Computation: 250 x $6 = $1,500

Date	Debit $	Credit $
Cash	2,100	
Share Capital		2,100
Explanation: Sold 300 common shares at $7 each to N. Greene.		

Computation: 300 x $7 = $2,100

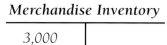

Cash		Merchandise Inventory	
2,000		3,000	
1,500			
2,100			
5,600			

Office Supplies		Office Equipment	
1,000		20,000	

Share Capital	
	26,000
	1,500
	2,100
	29,600

Kinshasa Incorporated
Balance Sheet
As at May 31, 2004

Assets		Liabilities	
Cash	$ 5,600		
Merchandise Inventory	3,000	**Shareholders' Equity**	
Office Supplies	1,000	Share Capital	
Office Equipment	20,000	Authorized common shares 250,000	
		Outstanding shares 5,750*	29,600
TOTAL	**29,600**	**TOTAL**	**29,600**

* 5,200 + 250 + 300 = 5,750

Solutions to Question Two

Alabaster Corporation General Journal

Date December 1, 2004	Debit $	Credit $
Organization Expense	$1,350	
Cash		$1,350
To record the organization expenses incurred for incorporation: Legal $1,000 Government $ 200 Printing $ 150 **TOTAL $1,350**		

Notes

_____
_____
_____
_____
_____
_____
_____
_____
_____
_____
_____
_____
_____
_____
_____
_____
_____

Notes

Notes

Chapter Two - Retaining Earnings

The Reason for This Chapter

In Chapter Two we link the corporate income statement to its balance sheet. The equity account "Retained Earnings" provides this bridge. It measures the profits earned by the firm since its inception. After completing this chapter you will understand how the Retained Earnings account enables us to distinguish equity obtained directly from shareholders versus that retained by making a profit.

This chapter also examines share issuance in greater detail. We introduce No-Par and Par-Value shares together with a demonstration of how to account for each. This process requires the introduction of a new equity account "Additional Paid-In Capital."

What Do You Already Know?

In this section of the chapter we ask you to complete a pre-test. It will get you thinking about what you already know about accounting. It will also serve as a link between what you learned in Chapter One and what you are about to learn in Chapter Two. After completing the pre-test, check your answers against the ones provided.

Question One

On November 1, 2004 Comco Incorporated was formed. 150,000 shares were authorized and 10% of that total were issued. Share distribution took place in the following manner:

Date	Name	Number	Price per Share
November 1, 2004	A. Booty	5,000	$5
November 1, 2004	B. Cohen	4,000	$5
November 1, 2004	C. Denis	3,000	$5
November 1, 2004	D. Every	2,000	$5
November 1, 2004	E. Front	?	$5

Determine the number of shares purchased by E. Front. Prepare the journal entry for November 1, 2004 using the space provided:

Number of shares issued to E. Front:

Comco Incorporated General Journal

Date		Debit $	Credit $

Computation:

Question Two

Discuss the main difference between a private and public corporation.

_____

_____

_____

_____

_____

_____

Question Three

The firm of Henderson & Bishop Ltd. is a corporation, not a partnership. How does the public know this?

_____

_____

_____

_____

_____

_____

Notes

_____

_____

_____

_____

_____

_____

_____

_____

_____

Answer to Question One

Number of shares issued to E. Front:
10% x 150,000 = 15,000 shares issued
5,000 + 4,000 + 3,000 + 2,000 = 14,000 issued to other shareholders
15,000 - 14,000 = 1,000 shares issued to E. Front

Comco Incorporated General Journal

Date November 1, 2004	Debit $	Credit $
Cash	75,000	
Share Capital		75,000
Sold 15,000 common shares at $5 each to:		
A. Booty 5,000		
B. Cohen 4,000		
C. Denis 3,000		
D. Every 2,000		
E. Front 1,000		
Total **15,000**		
Computation: 15,000 shares x $5 = $75,000		

Answer to Question Two

Corporations may be organized as either public or private. The distinction, noted in the Certificate of Incorporation, is based on whom will be able to purchase shares. Private corporations restrict the offering of their shares to a few individuals. Public corporations make their shares available to the general public. The shares of public corporations usually trade on an organized stock exchange. Most corporations begin privately, but as they grow they become public corporations.

Answer to Question Three

That's easy. While the name Henderson & Bishop may imply a partnership the term "Ltd." clearly informs us it is not. Whenever the word Limited (Ltd.), Corporation or Incorporated follows the company name we know the business is a corporation.

How This Chapter Relates to Other Chapters in This Book

The first chapter of this Volume examined share issuance with an introduction to the Shareholders' Equity account, Share Capital. We introduce a second equity account, Retained Earnings, in this chapter.

The Retained Earnings account provides the link between the corporate income statement and balance sheet. It shows how the corporation accumulates profit over time. In Chapter Two we account for distributions to shareholders. These are called dividends. As you will see, dividends reduce Retained Earnings. Chapter Three looks at the Statement of Retained Earnings, a fourth important financial statement.

What Are the Topics in This Chapter?

As you know, the main difference (from an accounting presentation perspective) between Corporations and the other forms of business can be found in the Equity Section of the balance sheet. This chapter links the income statement and balance sheet through the equity account, Retained Earnings. We also discuss share issuance in greater detail by considering par-value and no-par shares.

Topics Covered in Chapter Two   *Level of Importance*

Topic	Level of Importance
The Corporate Income Statement	
Net Income	***
Income Tax	***
Retaining Earnings	
Where Does Net Income Go?	***
Why Keep Earnings?	***
Journal Entries	
Using Retained Earnings	***
About Retained Earnings	
Accumulation	***
No-Par Value Stocks	
Issuing No-Par Shares	**
Par-Value Stocks	
Historical Meaning	**
Issuing Par-Value Shares	***
Additional Paid-In Capital	***
The Balance Sheet, again	**
Retaining Net Income	**

Legend

*   indicates a low level of importance

**   indicates a medium level of importance

***   indicates a high level of importance

The Corporate Income Statement

Net Income

The calculation of net income for a corporation is handled in much the same manner as with sole proprietorships and partnerships. Complete Exercise One. It provides a review of income statement preparation.

Now You Try It

Exercise One

The bookkeeper for Ignotics Incorporated has prepared an adjusted trial balance as at July 31, 2004:

Ignotics Incorporated
Adjusted Trial Balance
As at July 31, 2004

Account	Debit $	Credit $
Cash	8,375	
Accounts Receivable	400	
Supplies Inventory	1,000	
Equipment	2,000	
Accumulated Depreciation		50
Accounts Payable		1,500
Income Taxes Payable		68
Share Capital		10,000
Sales Revenue		2,275
Wages Expense	200	
Advertising Expense	300	
Supplies Expense	1,500	
Depreciation Expense	50	
Income Tax Expense (30%)	68	
TOTAL	**$13,893**	13,893

Use the space provided to prepare the income statement for
Ignotics Incorporated for the month ending July 31, 2004:

Ignotics Incorporated
Income Statement
For the month ended July 31, 2004

Sales Revenue

Expenses:

Total Expenses

Income before Taxes

Net Income

Answers

Answer to Exercise One

*Ignotics Incorporated
Income Statement
For the month ended July 31, 2004*

Sales Revenue		$2,275
Expenses:		
Wages Expense	$ 200	
Advertising Expense	300	
Supplies Expense	1,500	
Depreciation Expense	50	
Total Expenses		2,050
Income before Taxes		225
Income Tax Expense (30%)		68
Net Income		157

Income Tax

A corporation is an artificial entity that can enter into legal contracts in its own name. Therefore, the government taxes the income of a corporation. The corporation itself is responsible for any income taxes owing. Thus, the net income calculation must be net of the income tax expense.

The income tax rate for a corporation is determined by the nature of its business. This is unlike the other forms of business entities, where the income tax rate is based on the earnings of its owners.

The government provides a table of income tax rates for corporations. We will provide you with assumed tax rates, as needed.

The income tax expense appears on the income statement just before the net income line. We compute this expense by multiplying the taxable income by the tax rate. The tax expense is journalized through an adjusting entry and should appear in the adjusted trial balance. Review Exercise One, above. Verify the corporate income tax expense has been treated appropriately.

Retaining Earnings

Where Does Net Income Go?

The net income represents the profit earned by a corporation during the accounting period. Since this amount reflects the revenues in excess of the expenses, it must belong to shareholders. We place this profit on the balance sheet in the shareholders' equity section under a special account called Retained Earnings. This account name makes sense: we are retaining the earnings of the corporation and showing it as such.

With the other forms of business we simply adjusted the owner's capital account for any profits made, but corporations account for profits separately. The equity section of the balance sheet distinguishes money raised by issuing shares, (share capital), from profits earned by the corporation, (retained earnings).

If the corporation incurs a loss instead of earning a profit, the net loss reduces retained earnings. Again, the share capital account does not reflect the earnings of the corporation. The retained earnings account is adjusted for the profit or loss of the business.

Although Retained Earnings belongs to the shareholders it is not usually distributed entirely as cash to the shareholders. We discuss cash distributions to shareholders in Chapter Four.

Why Keep Earnings?

Keeping the profits in the corporation helps to finance its growth. Think about it. As more profits are earned and retained, the value of the shareholders' equity becomes larger. Since the balance sheet always balances, this increase must be offset by more assets or less liabilities. Making profits helps the firm expand by purchasing new assets, for example. Additionally, Retained Earnings could be used to reduce liabilities when there is sufficient cash on hand. Consider the following diagram:

Linking the Financial Statements

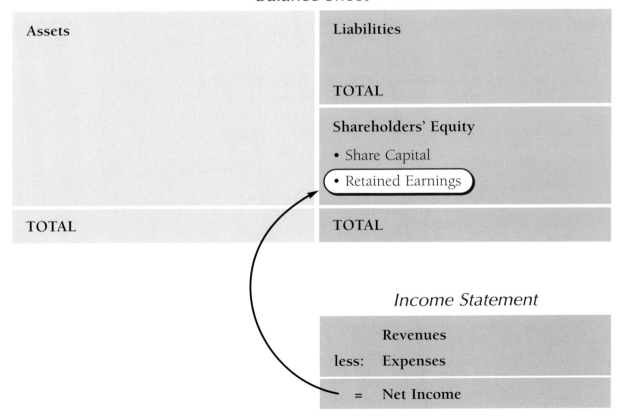

As we retain earnings the balance sheet values increase. Reporting this information communicates how well the business performed during an accounting period. This is true whether a profit or loss occurred. Using two separate equity accounts tells us whether changes in assets arise from selling more shares or retaining earnings. The distinction is important. Obviously, shareholders will not remain interested in a corporation that does not make profits and share issuance affects their ownership in the business.

Journal Entries

Using Retained Earnings

Do you remember closing entries? We simply close all the temporary accounts - the revenue and expense accounts - to income summary. At this point the entry to income summary equals net income or loss. We close corporate entries in exactly the same manner.

What happens to income summary? For sole proprietorships and partnerships we close it to the owner's capital account. Corporations handle this entry differently. We will close income summary to retained earnings, not to share capital. Remember, this enables us to track profit separately from share issuance.

Practice closing entries. Complete Exercise Two.

Now You Try It

Exercise Two

On July 31, 2004, the general ledger of Ignotics Incorporated shows the following:

Cash	Accounts Receivable	Supplies Inventory
8,375	400	1,000

Equipment	
2,000	

Accumulated Depreciation	
	50

Accounts Payable	
	1,500

Income Taxes Payable	
	68

Share Capital	
	10,000

Retained Earnings	

Sales Revenue	
	2,275

Wages Expense	
200	

Advertising Expense	
300	

Supplies Expense	
1,500	

Depreciation Expense	
50	

Income Tax Expense	
68	

Income Summary	

Prepare the necessary closing entries in the General Journal, provided below. Remember to close income summary to retained earnings. Post the entries to the appropriate ledger accounts.

Ignotics Incorporated General Journal

Date	Debit $	Credit $

Date	Debit $	Credit $

Date	Debit $	Credit $

Date	Debit $	Credit $

Date	Debit $	Credit $

Date	Debit $	Credit $

Date	Debit $	Credit $

Answers

Answer to Exercise Two

Ignotics Incorporated General Journal

Date July 31, 2004	Debit $	Credit $
Sales Revenue	2,275	
Income Summary		2,275
To close sales revenue to income summary.		

Date July 31, 2004	Debit $	Credit $
Income Summary	200	
Wages Expense		200
To close wages expense to income summary.		

Date July 31, 2004	Debit $	Credit $
Income Summary	300	
Advertising Expense		300
To close advertising expense to income summary.		

Date July 31, 2004	Debit $	Credit $
Income Summary	1,500	
Supplies Expense		1,500
To close supplies expense to income summary.		

Date July 31, 2004	Debit $	Credit $
Income Summary	50	
Depreciation Expense		50
To close depreciation expense to income summary.		

Date July 31, 2004	Debit $	Credit $
Income Summary	68	
Income Tax Expense		68
To close income tax expense to income summary.		

Date July 31, 2004	Debit $	Credit $
Income Summary	157	
Retained Earnings		157
To close income summary to retained earnings.		

Ignotics Incorporated General Ledger

Cash	
8,375	

Accounts Receivable	
400	

Supplies Inventory	
1,000	

Equipment	
2,000	

Accumulated Depreciation	
	50

Accounts Payable	
	1,500

Income Taxes Payable	
	68

Share Capital	
	10,000

Retained Earnings	
	157

Sales Revenue	
2,275	2,275
	0

Wages Expense	
200	200
0	

Advertising Expense	
300	300
0	

Supplies Expense	
1,500	1,500
0	

Income Summary	
	2,275
200	
300	
1,500	
50	
68	
	157
157	
0	

Depreciation Expense	
50	50
0	

Income Tax Expense	
68	68
0	

Notes

_____
_____
_____
_____
_____
_____
_____
_____
_____
_____
_____
_____
_____
_____
_____
_____
_____
_____
_____
_____
_____
_____
_____
_____
_____
_____
_____
_____
_____
_____
_____
_____
_____
_____

To ensure you remember the rest of the accounting process, complete Exercise Three.

Now You Try It

Exercise Three

Complete the accounting cycle for Ignotics Incorporated. Using the information from Exercise Two, prepare the July 31, 2004 balance sheet and post-closing trial balance. Assume that the Certificate of Incorporation for Ignotics shows that 100,000 common shares are authorized. Assume 20,000 shares are outstanding. Use the space provided below:

Ignotics Incorporated
Balance Sheet
As at _____

Assets	Liabilities
	TOTAL
	Shareholders' Equity
	TOTAL
TOTAL	**TOTAL**

Ignotics Incorporated
Post-Closing Trial Balance
As at _____

Account	Debit $	Credit $
TOTAL		

Answers

Answer to Exercise Three

Ignotics Incorporated
Balance Sheet
As at July 31, 2004

Assets		Liabilities	
Cash	$8,375	Accounts payable	1,500
Accounts Receivable	400	Income Taxes Payable	68
Supplies Inventory	1,000	**TOTAL**	**1,568**
Equipment	2,000		
Less: Accumulated Depreciation	(50)	**Shareholders' Equity**	
		Share Capital: 100,000 no-par common shares authorized; 20,000 shares issued	10,000
		Retained Earnings	157
		TOTAL	10,157
TOTAL	**11,725.00**	**TOTAL**	**11,725**

Ignotics Incorporated
Post-Closing Trial Balance
As at July 31, 2004

Account	Debit $	Credit $
Cash	8,375	
Accounts Receivable	400	
Supplies Inventory	1,000	
Equipment	2,000	
Accumulated Depreciation		50
Accounts Payable		1,500
Income Taxes Payable		68
Share Capital		10,000
Retained Earnings		157
TOTAL	11,775	11,775

About Retained Earnings

Accumulation

Did you notice that the retained earnings balance equals net income for Ignotics Incorporated? This is not the usual case. In fact, we only expect this will be true in the first period of operations. That is, retained earnings only equals net income in the first accounting period.

The retained earnings account shows the cumulative balance of earnings kept. For each additional accounting period we continue to add net income to the retained earnings balance. Net losses, of course, reduce retained earnings. Thus, the retained earnings account keeps track of total earnings since the company's inception. We say earnings accumulate in the retained earnings account or retained earnings is a cumulative account.

Try Exercise Four. It demonstrates how earnings accumulate.

Now You Try It

Exercise Four

On December 31, 2003 the retained earnings account for Memphis Limited has a balance of $23,450. The company enjoys success during the year 2004. The net income shown on the December 31, 2004 income statement is $18,940. What should be the retained earnings amount on the December 31, 2004 balance sheet.? Use the following equation as a guide:

retained earnings beginning **+** *net income* **=** *retained earnings ending*

Computation:

Answers

Answer to Exercise Four

Memphis Limited uses the calendar year for its accounting year. Thus, the accounting year begins each January 1st and ends on December 31st. Therefore, the retained earnings balance at the beginning of 2004 is the same as that at the end of 2003. So, the retained earnings balance on December 31, 2004 is:

$$23,450 + 18,940 = 42,390$$

We interpret this amount as representing $42,390 in profits that have been retained in the company since the inception of the firm.

No-Par Value Stocks

Issuing No-Par Shares

Good news! You already know all about no-par value shares. It was the topic of Chapter One. While we did not refer to them as such, the shares issued thus far have been no-par value. This means there is no pre-determined price attached to the shares. We record the value of no-par shares simply at the amount they are distributed for. The meaning of no-par becomes clear once you can account for par-value shares.

Par-Value Stocks

Historical Meaning

When a company applies for its certificate of incorporation, the company indicates both the number of authorized shares and the type of common shares. Two types of common shares exist: par-value and no-par value. Since we have already practiced accounting for no-par value shares, we will now examine accounting for par-value shares.

Par-value shares have a stated price. This price does not necessarily reflect that at which the shares are actually distributed. Historically, the par-value or stated price, represented a potential liability for shareholders. Today, this is no longer the case. Thus, the use of par-value shares has declined substantially. We have no need to further examine its legal meaning. However, we must be able to account for par-value shares because they are still in use.

Issuing Par-Value Shares

A corporation may have a par-value of $10 attached to each common share. This may not represent the price at which the shares are sold. The issued price of a share equals whatever shareholders are willing to pay for it. It is usual for the par-value to be a very low amount - such as $1.

When par-value shares exist, we must account for them. Whenever shares are sold, we record the par-value amount in the share capital account. Practice this idea. Try Exercise Five.

Now You Try It

Exercise Five

ABC Corporation has 500,000 authorized par-value common shares. The par-value of each share is $1. On May 4, 2004, the company issues 1,000 shares for cash, at a price of $5 each. Record the journal entry for the share issuance in the space provided below:

ABC Corporation General Journal

Date	Debit $	Credit $

Answers

Answer to Exercise Five

ABC Corporation General Journal

Date May 4, 2004	Debit $	Credit $
Cash	$5,000	
Share Capital		$1,000
To record the sale of 1,000 shares with par-value of $1 each.		

What is wrong with our journal entry? Debits do not equal credits! We never violate this basic accounting equation. Thus, this example is incomplete. We require another account to finish the transaction. We use a third equity account: Additional Paid-in Capital.

Additional Paid-In Capital

Generally, the corporation distributes common shares at a price greater than par value. We record the excess over par in the Additional Paid-In Capital account. We account for the par value amount in the Share Capital account.

Using this new account, we correct the answer for Exercise Five. It should look like this:

ABC Corporation General Journal

Date May 4, 2004	Debit $	Credit $
Cash	$5,000	
Share Capital		$1,000
Additional Paid-In Capital		$4,000
To record the sale of 1,000 shares with par-value of $1 each, sold for $5 each.		

Computation: 1,000 x ($5 - $1) = $4,000

Now the debits equal credits and the entire $5,000 has been accounted for. Notice we record the par value per share of $1 in the Share Capital account and the excess over par ($5 - $1) = $4 per share in the Additional Paid-In Capital account.

The Balance Sheet, Again

We sometimes refer to Additional Paid-In Capital as Contributed Surplus. The meaning is the same. We show this account on the balance sheet immediately following the Share Capital amount.

Let's use ABC Corporation from Exercise Five above. Assuming it has $2,800 in Retained Earnings at the end of the accounting period, the equity section of the balance sheet looks like this:

Shareholders' Equity

Share Capital		
Authorized	500,000 common shares at $1 par each	
Outstanding	1,000 common shares	**$1,000**
Additional Paid-In Capital		**$4,000**
Retained Earnings		**$2,800**
TOTAL Shareholders' Equity		**$7,800**

Retaining Net Income

Whether common shares are authorized as par-value or no-par value has no impact on the way we account for retained earnings. The classification makes no difference because we always retain net income as retained earnings. Thus, we close the full amount of net income from the income statement, via income summary, to the retained earnings account on the balance sheet.

Practice dealing with par-value shares. Try Exercise Six.

Now You Try It

Exercise Six

The Certificate of Incorporation for Colors Limited states 1,000,000, $2 par-value shares are authorized. Shares are distributed in the following manner:

Date	Name	Number	Price per Share
September 1, 2004	U. N. Owen	2,000	$10
September 1, 2004	T. Star	1,800	$11
September 1, 2004	J. Ado	4,200	$9.50
September 1, 2004	L. Singh	3,000	$12

Record the necessary journal entries. Prepare the shareholders'
equity section of the balance sheet as at September 30, 2004.
Assume no other transactions took place during the month. Use
$10,300 for the Retained Earnings balance. We have provided the
appropriate spaces below:

Colors Limited General Journal

Date	Debit $	Credit $

Computation:

Date	Debit $	Credit $

Computation:

Date	Debit $	Credit $

Computation:

Date	Debit $	Credit $

Computation:

Colors Limited
Shareholders' Equity
As at _____

Share Capital		
Additional Paid-In Capital		
Retained Earnings		
TOTAL Shareholders' Equity		

Answers

Answer to Exercise Six

Colors Limited General Journal

Date September 1, 2004	Debit $	Credit $
Cash	$20,000	
Share Capital		$4,000
Additional Paid-In Capital		$16,000
To record the sale of 2,000 shares with par-value of $2 each, sold to U. N. Owen for $10 each.		

Computation: 2,000 x $2 = $ 4,000

             2,000 x ($10 - $2) = $16,000

             2,000 x ($10 - $2) = $16,000

                 total = $20,000

Date September 5, 2004	Debit $	Credit $
Cash	$19,800	
Share Capital		$3,600
Additional Paid-In Capital		$16,200
To record the sale of 1,800 shares with par-value of $2 each, sold to T. Star for $11 each.		

Computation: 1,800 x $2 = $ 3,600

             1,800 x ($11 - $2) = $16,200

                 total = $19,800

Date September 13, 2004	Debit $	Credit $
Cash	$39,900	
Share Capital		$8,400
Additional Paid-In Capital		$31,500
To record the sale of 4,200 shares with par-value of $2 each, sold to J. Ado for $9.50 each.		

Computation: $4,200 \times \$2 = \$\ 8,400$

$4,200 \times (\$9.50 - \$2) = \$31,500$

$total = \$39,900$

Date September 22, 2004	Debit $	Credit $
Cash	$36,000	
Share Capital		$6,000
Additional Paid-In Capital		$30,000
To record the sale of 3,000 shares with par-value of $2 each, sold to L. Singh for $12 each.		

Computation: $3,000 \times \$2 = \$\ 6,000$

$3,000 \times (\$12 - \$2) = \$30,000$

$total = \$36,000$

Did you notice the shares are distributed at many different prices? Attempts to justify share price are beyond the scope of this book. However, we recognize the share price can be any amount and will usually be greater than par value.

Colors Limited
Shareholders' Equity
As at September 30, 2004

Share Capital		
Authorized	1,000,000 common shares at $2 par each	
Outstanding	11,000 common shares	$ 22,000
Additional Paid-In Capital		$ 93,700
Retained Earnings		$ 10,300
TOTAL Shareholders' Equity		$126,000

What You Have Learned in This Chapter

Chapter Two introduces two new equity accounts: Retained Earnings and Additional Paid-In Capital. The latter of these is used only when the Certificate of Incorporation specifies the common shares have a par-value.

The Retained Earnings account provides a link between the balance sheet and income statement. When recording the entries at the end of the accounting cycle we close net income to income summary. Income summary is closed to retained earnings. This is true whether the shares are par or no-par value.

Par-value shares contain a stated share price. While the meaning of par-value no longer has any significance, we must account for both the stated price and the amount in excess of par in separate equity accounts. We use Additional Paid-In Capital to reflect the share price in excess of the par value.

Important Terms in This Chapter

Accumulation: building-up. The retained earnings accounts accumulates earnings.

Additional Paid-In Capital: the complementary account to share capital for par-value shares. The excess amount over par is recorded here.

Contributed Surplus: another name for Additional Paid-In Capital.

Income Summary: a temporary account used to close revenues and expenses. We close income summary to retained earnings.

No-Par Value Shares: shares without a par value attached. We record the full distribution amount to share capital.

Par-Value Shares: shares with a specific par value attached. We record the par value in the share capital account and the excess in additional paid-in capital.

Retaining: keeping

Retained Earnings: the shareholders' equity account that reflects the accumulated profits and losses earned by the corporation since its inception.

Should You Move on to the Next Chapter?

Now it's time to check and see how comfortable you are with your new knowledge. Perform the Self-Test to verify whether you should move on, or go back and review the information contained in this chapter.

Self-Test for Chapter Two

Question One

What effect does a net loss have on the Retained Earnings account?

_____
_____
_____
_____
_____

Question Two

What is the difference between par-value and no-par value shares?

_____
_____
_____
_____
_____

Question Three

A group of business people have received a certificate of incorporation to operate a business called General Business Limited. They were authorized to issue a total of 50,000 common shares, each with a par-value of $3. Record each of the following transactions in the General Journal. Use the space provided.

Transactions:

On February 5, 2004, 1,000 shares were sold to J. George for $20,000 cash.

On February 11, 2004, 500 shares were issued to B. Petty in exchange for machinery valued at $9,000.

On February 21, 2004, 6,000 shares were issued to V. Wang in exchange for a building valued at $120,000.

General Business Limited General Journal

Date	Debit $	Credit $

Computation:

Date	Debit $	Credit $

Computation:

Date	Debit $	Credit $

Computation:

Answers to Self-Test for Chapter Two

Answer to Question One

We close net income to retained earnings via income summary. A profit will increase the retained earnings account. Thus, a net loss reduces retained earnings. This reduction appropriately shows the decline in shareholders' equity due to the loss incurred for operating the business during that accounting period.

Answer to Question Two

Par, or stated value means each distributed share must be recorded in the Share Capital account at this value. When the distributed shares are sold above their par value, we record the excess in the Additional Paid-In Capital account. No-par value shares do not require this extra journal entry. The entire selling price of each share is recorded in the share capital account.

Answer to Question Three

General Business Limited General Journal

Date February 5, 2004	Debit $	Credit $
Cash	$20,000	
Share Capital		$3,000
Additional Paid-In Capital		$17,000
Sold 1,000 $3 par value shares for $20 each to J. George.		

Computation: 20,000 ÷ 1,000 = $20 per share issue price

1,000 x $3   = $ 3,000

1,000 x ($20 - $3) = $17,000

total   = $20,000

Date February 11, 2004	Debit $	Credit $
Machinery	$9,000	
Share Capital		$1,500
Additional Paid-In Capital		$7,500
Issued 500 $3 par value shares for $18 each to B. Petty in exchange for $9,000 of machinery.		

Computation: 9,000 ÷ 500 = $18 per share issue price
500 x $3   = $1,500
500 x ($18 - $3) = $7,500
total   = $9,000

Date February 21, 2004	Debit $	Credit $
Building	$120,000	
Share Capital		$18,000
Additional Paid-In Capital		$102,000
Issued 6,000 $3 par value shares for $20 each to V. Wang in exchange for a building valued at $120,000.		

Computation: 120,000 ÷ 6,000 = $20 per share issue price
6,000 x $3   = $ 18,000
6,000 x ($20 - $3) = $102,000
total   = $120,000

Practice Problems for Chapter Two

Question One

On December 31, 2000, Zippy Inc. completed its first year of operations. A profit of $15,480 was earned for the year. Since that time the company has enjoyed some success. The company's income statement for each year shows the following:

Date	Net Income (Loss)
December 31, 2001	$12,840
December 31, 2002	16,350
December 31, 2003	(2,420)
December 31, 2004	20,350

What is the opening balance in the Retained Earnings account on January 1, 2005? What does this number mean?

Computation:

Question Two

On May 31, 2004, the Adjusted Trial Balance for Bee Good Ltd. shows the following:

Bee Good Ltd.
Adjusted Trial Balance
As at May 31, 2004

Account	Debit $	Credit $
Cash	11,004	
Accounts Receivable	52,000	
Office Supplies Inventory	5,000	
Building	240,000	
Accumulated Depreciation		35,000
Accounts Payable		20,000
Wages Payable		15,000
Share Capital		155,000
Retained Earnings		42,000
Sales Revenue		89,275
Wages Expense	30,520	
Heat & Light Expense	3,500	
Office Supplies Expense	2,500	
Depreciation Expense	1,500	
Income Tax Expense (20%)	10,251	
TOTAL	$356,275	356,275

The company is authorized to issue 200,000 no-par common shares, of which 40,000 are outstanding.

On the same date, but prior to closing entries the General Ledger shows the following account balances:

Cash		Accounts Receivable		Office Supplies Inventory	
11,004		52,000		5,000	

Building		Accumulated Depreciation	
240,000			35,000

Accounts Payable		Wages Payable		Share Capital	
	20,000		15,000		155,000

Retained Earnings	
	42,000

Sales Revenue		Wages Expense		Heat & Light Expense	
	89,275	30,520		3,500	

Office Supplies Expense		Depreciation Expense		Income Tax Expense	
2,500		1,500		10,251	

Income Summary	

Required:

Prepare the income statement for the month ending May 31, 2004 and the balance sheet as at May 31, 2004 for Bee Good Limited. Record and post the closing entries. Prepare a post closing trial balance. Use the ledger space provided above and the spaces provided below:

Bee Good Ltd.
Income Statement
For the _____

Sales Revenue		
Expenses:		
Total Expenses		
Income before Taxes		
Net Income		

Bee Good Ltd.
Balance Sheet
As at _____

Assets	Liabilities
	TOTAL
	Shareholders' Equity
	TOTAL
TOTAL	TOTAL

Bee Good Ltd. General Journal

Date	Debit $	Credit $

Date	Debit $	Credit $

Date	Debit $	Credit $

Date	Debit $	Credit $

Date	Debit $	Credit $

Date	Debit $	Credit $

Date	Debit $	Credit $

Bee Good Ltd.
Post-Closing Trial Balance
As at _____

Account	Debit $	Credit $
TOTAL		

Solutions to Practice Problems for Chapter Two

Solutions to Question One

Simply add the net income or subtract net loss for each year. In the first year the beginning balance was zero:

$0 + $15,480 + $12,840 + $16,350 - $2,420 + $20,350 = $62,600.

The Retained Earnings balance on January 1, 2005 is $62,600. We interpret this to mean that $62,600 in profits have been retained in the company since its inception.

Solution to Question Two

Bee Good Ltd.
Income Statement
For the month ended May 31, 2004

Sales Revenue		**$89,275**
Expenses:		
Wages Expense	$30,520	
Heat & Light Expense	3,500	
Office Supplies Expense	2,500	
Depreciation Expense	1,500	
Total Expenses		38,020
Income before Taxes		51,255
Income Tax Expense (20%)		10,251
Net Income		41,004

Bee Good Ltd.
Balance Sheet
As at May 31, 2004

Assets		**Liabilities**	
Cash	$11,004	Accounts payable	20,000
Accounts Receivable	52,000	Wages Payable	15,000
Office Supplies Inventory	5,000	**TOTAL**	**35,000**
Building	240,000		
Less: Accumulated Depreciation	(35,000)	**Shareholders' Equity**	
		Share Capital: 200,000 no-par common shares authorized; 40,000 shares issued	155,000
		Retained Earnings	83,004
		TOTAL	**238,004**
TOTAL	**273,004**	**TOTAL**	**273,004**

Bee Good ltd. General Journal

Date May 31, 2004	Debit $	Credit $
Sales revenue	$89,275	
Income Summary		$89,275
To close sales revenue to income summary		

Date May 31, 2004	Debit $	Credit $
Income Summary	$30,520	
Wages Expense		$30,520
To close wages expense to income summary		

Date May 31, 2004	Debit $	Credit $
Income Summary	$3,500	
Heat & Light Expense		$3,500
To close heat & light expense to income summary		

Date May 31, 2004	Debit $	Credit $
Income Summary	$2,500	
Office Supplies Expense		$2,500
To close office supplies expense to income summary		

Date May 31, 2004	Debit $	Credit $
Income Summary	$1,500	
Depreciation Expense		$1,500
To close depreciation expense to income summary		

Date May 31, 2004	Debit $	Credit $
Income Summary	$10,251	
Income tax Expense		$10,251
To close income tax expense to income summary		

Date May 31, 2004	Debit $	Credit $
Income Summary	$41,004	
Retained Earnings		$41,004
To close income summary to retained earnings		

Bee Good Ltd. General Ledger

Cash	
11,004	

Accounts Receivable	
52,000	

Office Supplies Inventory	
5,000	

Building	
240,000	

Accumulated Depreciation	
	35,000

Accounts Payable	
	20,000

Wages Payable	
	15,000

Share Capital	
	155,000

Retained Earnings	
	42,000
	41,004
	83,004

Sales Revenue	
89,275	89,275
0	

Wages Expense	
30,520	30,520
0	

Heat & Light Expense	
3,500	3,500
0	

Office Supplies Expense	
2,500	2,500
0	

Depreciation Expense	
1,500	1,500
0	

Income Tax Expense	
10,251	10,251
0	

Income Summary	
	89,275
30,520	
3,500	
2,500	
1,500	
10,251	
	41,004
41,004	
	0

Bee Good Ltd.
Post-Closing Trial Balance
As at May 31, 2004

Account	Debit $	Credit $
Cash	11,004	
Accounts Receivable	52,000	
Office Supplies Inventory	5,000	
Building	240,000	
Accumulated Depreciation		35,000
Accounts Payable		20,000
Wages Payable		15,000
Share Capital		155,000
Retained Earnings		83,004
TOTAL	308,004	308,004

Notes

Notes

Accounting for Corporations

Chapter Three - Practicing with Shareholders' Equity

The Reason for This Chapter

Can you complete the nine steps in the accounting cycle, for a corporation? This chapter gives you the opportunity to do so. You must rely on the accounting knowledge gained in Volumes One, Two and Three in addition to Chapters One and Two of this Volume.

This Chapter consists of two separate case studies, each involving a different company. Each company operates a business, but they need help with their books. As an accountant, you will provide this aid.

In each case we will provide you with transactions and dates, along with other pertinent information. To guide you through the accounting process we have provided blank forms for each case. All you must do is complete the forms provided!

What Do You Already Know?

In this section of the chapter we ask you to complete a pre-test. It will get you thinking about what you already know about accounting. It will also serve as a quick review of Chapters One and Two.

If you have difficulties with the pre-test, you should go back and review the previous chapters. After completing the pre-test, check your answers against the ones provided. If they are correct, then complete the cases in this chapter.

Question One

The year-end for Surplus Incorporated is each March 31st. The shareholders' equity section of the balance sheet as at April 1, 2004 is provided below:

Surplus Incorporated
Shareholders' Equity
As at April 1, 2004

Share Capital		
Authorized	800,000 common shares at $1 par each	
Outstanding	30,000 common shares	$ 30,000
Additional Paid-In Capital		$ 54,000
Retained Earnings		$ 82,800
TOTAL Shareholders' Equity		$166,800

The company reported net income of $16,560 for the fiscal year ended March 31, 2004. Recall the fiscal year has the same number of days as the calendar year, but does not necessarily begin each January 1st nor end each December 31st.

If the net income of Surplus Incorporated was the same this fiscal year, as for each year since its inception, in what year did the company begin business?

_____

_____

_____

_____

_____

_____

Computation:

Question Two

Use the information from Question One for Surplus Incorporated. What is the average price at which it sold each outstanding share?

_____
_____
_____
_____
_____
_____

What is the average investment of each shareholder?

_____
_____
_____
_____
_____
_____

Computation:

Answer to Question One

The retained earnings equals $82,800. Net income has been $16,560 for each fiscal year. The net income for the fiscal year ended March 31, 2004 must be included in the balance sheet dated April 1, 2004. Thus, the company has operated for:

$$\$82,800 \div \$16,560 = 5 \ years$$

Thus, 2004 - 5 = 1999. The company began operations in 1999. Since its fiscal year ends each March 31st, it must begin the next year each April 1st. So, Surplus Incorporated began operations on April 1st, 1999. Retained earnings were zero at that time. The first net income was posted on March 31st, 2000 for the first fiscal year. Surplus Incorporated continued to show the same net income for each of the following four fiscal years; 2001, 2002, 2003 and 2004.

Answer to Question Two

The average share price is determined by simply dividing the total amount raised from selling shares by the number of outstanding shares. For Surplus Incorporated:

$30,000 + $54,000 = $84,000 in total was raised from selling shares. Since 30,000 shares were sold, the average price of each share is:

$$\$84,000 \div 30,000 = \$2.80$$

In addition, the company has retained earnings of $82,800 since its inception. Thus, investors have invested a total of $82,800 + $84,000 = $166,800 in the company. With 30,000 shares outstanding, the average investment is:

$$\$166,800 \div 30,000 = \$5.56$$

That is, $2.80 came directly from selling shares and the remainder ($5.56 - $2.80 = $2.76) came from retaining profits.

How This Chapter Relates to Other Chapters in This Book

This chapter consists of two cases. Each case will require you to account for a corporation during a particular accounting period. You must use all the steps in the accounting cycle to complete each case.

Each case will allow you to practice the knowledge gained in Chapters One and Two. In addition, you will also rely upon the expertise gained in Volumes One, Two and Three. Should you encounter any difficulties, we encourage you to review the previously covered material.

Topics Covered in Chapter Three

Case One
Will Knott Incorporated

Case Two
Havealot Limited

Case One

Will Knott Incorporated

Will Knott, a sole proprietor, received a certificate of incorporation allowing him to re-organize his business as a private corporation. The name is Will Knott Incorporated. The accounts of his proprietorship were exchanged for common shares.

Will Knott Incorporated is authorized to issue 1,000,000 common shares with a par value of $1 each. The accounts of the sole proprietorship, Will Knott Company, showed the following balances immediately prior to the incorporation:

Will Knott Incorporated

Account Title	Debit $	Credit $
Cash	19,000	
Office Supplies	2,000	
Equipment	15,000	
Building	200,000	
Will Knott, Capital		236,000

On August 31, 2004 the accounts of the sole proprietorship were closed.

During the month of September, 2004, the following transactions occurred:

Date	Transaction	Amount
Sept. 1	Issued shares to Will Knott in exchange for the assets of Will Knott Company.	$20 each
Sept. 1	Issued 50 shares to L. Begal at $20 each in exchange for legal services to set up the corporation.	$ 1,000
Sept. 5	Generated sales revenues by performing services, on account. The receivable is due next month.	$ 4,500
Sept. 7	Paid $2,400 cash for a 12 month insurance policy. Coverage began September 1, 2004.	$ 2,400
Sept. 8	Advertised services on local radio show. Paid cash.	$ 1,400
Sept. 10	Issued shares at $25 each to R. Teare, for cash.	$ 1,000
Sept. 11	Incurred maintenance expense for the equipment. Paid cash	$ 2,600
Sept. 13	Generated sales revenues by performing services, on account. The receivable is due next month.	$ 2,720
Sept. 15	Borrowed money from the bank. Interest is due on the 15th day of each month. The interest rate is 8% per year. The loan is due in one year.	$20,000
Sept. 15	Paid employees for work performed during the first fifteen days of the month.	$ 3,000
Sept. 20	Purchased land, for cash	$20,000
Sept. 25	Purchased office supplies, on account. The account is due in 30 days.	$ 1,000
Sept. 26	Incurred miscellaneous expenses. Paid cash.	$875
Sept. 28	Generated sales revenues by performing services. Received cash.	$ 2,200
Sept. 30	Paid employees for work performed during the last fifteen days of the month.	$ 3,000
Sept. 30	Received the utilities bill, for the month of September. It will be paid next month. It is recorded as an accounts payable.	$650

Additional Information:

Insurance should be expensed for one whole month.

The interest incurred on the bank loan for September is for 1/2 a month.

There are $1,200 worth of office supplies left in inventory at the end of September.

The equipment and building are depreciated using the straight-line method. The equipment has an expected life of 5 years with zero salvage value. The building has an expected life of 20 years with a disposal value of $50,000. Use a separate accumulated depreciation account on the balance sheet for each of these assets, but only one depreciation expense account.

If revenues exceed expenses, taxes will be charged at a rate of 25% on the difference. Any taxes owed will be paid at the end of December, 2004.

Required:

Complete the accounting cycle for Will Knott Incorporated for the month of September, from beginning to end. This entails 9 steps:

1. Analyze each transaction.

2. Prepare the journal entries.

3. Post them to the ledger.

4. Prepare a trial balance.

5. Prepare the necessary adjusting entries and post them to the ledger.

6. Prepare an adjusted trial balance.

7. Prepare the income statement and balance sheet.

8. Prepare the closing entries and post them to the ledger.

9. Prepare a post-closing trial balance.

Use the space provided below.

Will Knott Incorporated - General Journal

Date		Debit $	Credit $
Explanation:			

Computation:

Date		Debit $	Credit $
Explanation:			

Computation:

Date		Debit $	Credit $
Explanation:			

Date	Debit $	Credit $
Explanation:		

Date	Debit $	Credit $
Explanation:		

Date	Debit $	Credit $
Explanation:		

Computation:

Date	Debit $	Credit $
Explanation:		

Date	Debit $	Credit $
Explanation:		

Date	Debit $	Credit $
Explanation:		

Date	Debit $	Credit $
Explanation:		

Date	Debit $	Credit $
Explanation:		

Date	Debit $	Credit $
Explanation:		

Date	Debit $	Credit $
Explanation:		

Date	Debit $	Credit $
Explanation:		

Date	Debit $	Credit $
Explanation:		

Date	Debit $	Credit $
Explanation:		

Will Knott Incorporated - General Ledger

Note: use for all entries, including closing.

Cash   Accounts Receivable   Office Supplies

Prepaid Insurance   Equipment   Accum. Dep'n. (equip.)

Building   Accum. Dep'n. (building)   Land

Accounts Payable

Bank Loan

Interest Payable

Income Taxes Payable

Share Capital

Additional Paid-In Capital

Retained Earnings

Sales Revenue

Insurance Expense

Advertising Expense

Maintenance Expense

Interest Expense

Organization Expenses

Wages Expense

Office Supplies Expense

Miscellaneous Expense

Utilities Expense

Depreciation Expense

Income Tax Expense

Income Summary

Will Knott Incorporated
Trial Balance
As at September 30, 2004

Account	Debit $	Credit $
TOTAL		

Note: only include ledger accounts that have a balance in the trial balance.

Will Knott Incorporated General Journal - Adjusting Entries

Date	Debit $	Credit $
Explanation:		

Computation:

Date	Debit $	Credit $
Explanation:		

Computation:

Date	Debit $	Credit $
Explanation:		

Computation:

Date	Debit $	Credit $
Explanation:		

Computation:

Will Knott Incorporated
Adjusted Trial Balance
As at September 30, 2004

Account	Debit $	Credit $
TOTAL		

Note: only include ledger accounts that have a balance in the adjusted trial balance.

Will Knott Incorporated
Income Statement
For the month ended September 30, 2004

Sales Revenue		
Expenses:		
Total Expenses		
Net Income (Loss) for the month		

Notes

_____
_____
_____
_____
_____
_____
_____
_____
_____

Will Knott Incorporated
Balance Sheet
As at September 30, 2004

Assets	Liabilities
	TOTAL (Liabilities)
	Shareholders' Equity
	TOTAL (Shareholders' Equity)
TOTAL (Assets)	**TOTAL** (Liabilities and Shareholders' Equity)

Will Knott General Journal - Closing Entries

Date	Debit $	Credit $
Explanation:		

Date	Debit $	Credit $
Explanation:		

Date	Debit $	Credit $
Explanation:		

Date	Debit $	Credit $
Explanation:		

Date	Debit $	Credit $
Explanation:		

Date	Debit $	Credit $
Explanation:		

Date	Debit $	Credit $
Explanation:		

Date	Debit $	Credit $
Explanation:		

Date	Debit $	Credit $
Explanation:		

Date	Debit $	Credit $
Explanation:		

Date	Debit $	Credit $
Explanation:		

Date	Debit $	Credit $
Explanation:		

Will Knott Incorporated
Post-Closing Trial Balance
As at September 30, 2004

Account	Debit $	Credit $
TOTAL		

Notes

_____

_____

_____

_____

_____

_____

_____

_____

_____

_____

Solutions to Case One

Will Knott Incorporated - General Journal

Date September 1, 2004	Debit $	Credit $
Cash	19,000	
Office Supplies	2,000	
Equipment	15,000	
Building	200,000	
Share Capital		11,800
Additional Paid-In Capital		224,200
Explanation: Issued 11,800 par-value $1 shares issued at $20 each, in exchange for assets.		

Computation: 236,000 ÷ $20 = 11,800 shares issued
                11,800 x $1 = $11,800
                11,800 x ($20 - $1) = $224,000

Date September 1, 2004	Debit $	Credit $
Organization Expenses	1,000	
Share Capital		50
Additional Paid-In Capital		950
Explanation: Issued 50 par-value $1 shares to L. Begal at $20 each, in exchange for legal services.		

Computation: 1,000 ÷ 50 = $20 per share issue price
                50 x $1 = $50
                50 x ($20 - $1) = $950

Date September 5, 2004	Debit $	Credit $
Accounts Receivable	4,500	
Sales Revenue		4,500
Explanation: To record sales earned, on account.		

Date September 7, 2004	Debit $	Credit $
Prepaid Insurance	2,400	
Cash		2,400
Explanation: To record the payment for a twelve-month insurance policy. Coverage began Sept. 1, 2004.		

Date September 8, 2004	Debit $	Credit $
Advertising Expense	1,400	
Cash		1,400
Explanation: To record the purchase of a radio advertisement, for cash.		

Date September 10, 2004	Debit $	Credit $
Cash	1,000	
Share Capital		40
Additional Paid-In Capital		960
Explanation: Issued 40 par-value $1 shares to R. Teare at $25 each, for cash.		

Computation: $1,000 ÷ $25 = 40 shares
40 x $1 = $40
40 x ($25 - $1) = $960

Date September 11, 2004	Debit $	Credit $
Maintenance Expense	2,600	
Cash		2,600
Explanation: To record maintenance expense incurred.		

Date September 13, 2004	Debit $	Credit $
Accounts Receivable	2,720	
Sales Revenue		2,720
Explanation: To record sales revenue on account.		

Date September 15, 2004	Debit $	Credit $
Cash	20,000	
Bank Loan		20,000
Explanation: To record receipt of bank loan. Interest due monthly at 8%. Loan due in one year.		

Date September 15, 2004	Debit $	Credit $
Wages Expense	3,000	
Cash		3,000
Explanation: To record wage payment to employees.		

Date September 20, 2004	Debit $	Credit $
Land	20,000	
Cash		20,000
Explanation: To record the purchase of land.		

Date September 25, 2004	Debit $	Credit $
Office Supplies	1,000	
Accounts Payable		1,000
Explanation: To record the purchase of office supplies on account.		

Date September 26, 2004	Debit $	Credit $
Miscellaneous Expense	875	
Cash		875
Explanation: To record the payment of miscellaneous expenses for cash.		

Date September 28, 2004	Debit $	Credit $
Cash	2,200	
Sales Revenue		2,200
Explanation: To record cash sales earned.		

Date September 30, 2004	Debit $	Credit $
Wages Expenses	3,000	
Cash		3,000
Explanation: To record wage payment to employees.		

Date September 30, 2004	Debit $	Credit $
Utilities Expenses	650	
Accounts payable		650
Explanation: To record utilities expense, not yet paid.		

Will Knott Incorporated - General Ledger

Note: use for all entries, including closing.

Cash	
19,000	2,400
1,000	1,400
20,000	2,600
2,200	3,000
	20,000
	875
	3,000
8,925	

Accounts Receivable	
4,500	
2,720	
7,220	

Office Supplies	
2,000	
1,000	
3,000	
	1,800
1,200	

Prepaid Insurance	
2,400	
	200
2,200	

Equipment	
15,000	

Accum. Dep'n. (equip.)	
	250

Building	
200,000	

Accum. Dep'n. (building)	
	625

Land	
20,000	

Accounts Payable		Bank Loan		Interest Payable	
	1,000		20,000		67
	650				
	1,650				

Income Taxes Payable		Share Capital	
			11,800
			50
			40
			11,890

Additional Paid-In Capital		Retained Earnings		Sales Revenue	
	224,200	6,047			4,500
	950				2,720
	960				2,200
	226,110			9,420	9,420
					0

Insurance Expense		Advertising Expense		Maintenance Expense		Interest Expense	
200	200	1,400	1,400	2,600	2,600	67	67
0		0		0		0	

Organization Expenses		Wages Expense		Office Supplies Expense		Miscellaneous Expense	
1,000	1,000	3,000		1,800	1,800	875	875
0		3,000		0		0	
		6,000	6,000				
		0					

Utilities Expense		Depreciation Expense		Income Tax Expense	
650	650	875	875		
0		0			

Income Summary

1,400	9,420
2,600	
1,000	
6,000	
875	
650	
200	
67	
1,800	
875	
6,047	
	6,047
0	

Will Knott Incorporated
Trial Balance
As at September 30, 2004

Account	Debit $	Credit $
Cash	8,925	
Accounts Receivable	7,220	
Office Supplies	3,000	
Prepaid Insurance	2,400	
Equipment	15,000	
Building	200,000	
Land	20,000	
Accounts Payable		1,650
Bank Loan		20,000
Share Capital		11,890
Additional Paid-In Capital		226,110
Sales Revenue		9,420
Advertising Expense	1,400	
Maintenance Expense	2,600	
Organization Expense	1,000	
Wages Expense	6,000	
Miscellaneous Expense	875	
Utilities Expense	650	
TOTAL	269,070	269,070

Will Knott Incorporated General Journal - Adjusting Entries

Date September 30, 2004	Debit $	Credit $
Insurance Expense	200	
Prepaid Insurance		200
Explanation: To record insurance expense for the month of September.		

Computation: $2,400 ÷ 12 months = $200 per month

Date September 30, 2004	Debit $	Credit $
Interest Expense	67	
Interest Payable		67
Explanation: To record interest expense for the month of September incurred but not yet paid.		

Computation: $20,000 x 8% = $1,600 per year
$1,600 ÷ 12 months = $133.33 per month
$133.33 ÷ 2 = $66.67 or $67 for 1/2 month.

Date September 30, 2004	Debit $	Credit $
Office Supplies Expense	1,800	
Office Supplies		1,800
Explanation: To record office supplies used during the month of September.		

Computation: $3,000 - $1,200 = $1,800 in office supplies used during September.

Date September 30, 2004	Debit $	Credit $
Depreciation Expense	875	
Accumulated Depreciation - Equipment		250
Accumulated Depreciation - Building		625
Explanation: To record depreciation expenses for the month of September.		

Computation: Equipment: ($15,000 - 0) ÷ 5 years = $3,000 per year
$3,000 ÷ 12 months = $250 per month

Building: ($200,000 - $50,000) ÷ 20 years = $7,500 per year
$7,500 ÷ 12 months = $625 per month

Total: $250 + $625 = $875

Income Taxes: *Since expenses exceed revenues there will be no income tax expense for the month. Using the trial balance and adjusting entries, we compute the net loss:*

$9,420 - 1,400 - 2,600 - 1,000 - 6,000 - 875 - 650 - 200 - 67 - 1,800 - 875 = -$6,047

Will Knott Incorporated
Adjusted Trial Balance
As at September 30, 2004

Account	Debit $	Credit $
Cash	8,925	
Accounts Receivable	7,220	
Office Supplies	1,200	
Prepaid Insurance	2,200	
Equipment	15,000	
Accumulated Depreciation - Equipment		250
Building	200,000	
Accumulated Depreciation - Building		625
Land	20,000	
Accounts Payable		1,650
Bank Loan		20,000
Interest Payable		67
Share Capital		11,890
Additional Paid-In Capital		226,110
Sales Revenue		9,420
Advertising Expense	1,400	
Maintenance Expense	2,600	
Organization Expense	1,000	
Wages Expense	6,000	
Miscellaneous Expense	875	
Utilities Expense	650	
Insurance Expense	200	
Interest Expense	67	
Office Supplies Expense	1,800	
Depreciation Expense	875	
TOTAL	270,012	270,012

Will Knott Incorporated
Income Statement
For the month ended September 30, 2004

Sales Revenue		$9,420
Expenses:		
Advertising	$1,400	
Maintenance	2,600	
Organization	1,000	
Wages	6,000	
Utilities	650	
Insurance	200	
Interest	67	
Office Supplies	1,800	
Depreciation	875	
Miscellaneous	875	
Total Expenses		15,467
Net Income (Loss) for the month		(6,047)

Will Knott Incorporated
Balance Sheet
As at September 30, 2004

Assets		Liabilities	
Cash	$8,925	Accounts payable	1,650
Accounts Receivable	7,220	Interest Payable	67
Office Supplies	1,200	Bank Loan	20,000
Prepaid Insurance	2,200	**TOTAL** (Liabilities)	21,717
Equipment	15,000		
Less: Accumulated Depreciation		**Shareholders' Equity**	
Equipment	(250)	Share Capital: 1,000,000	11,890
Building	200,000	par-value $1 common shares	
Less: Accumulated Depreciation		authorized, 11,890 shares issued	
building	(625)	Additional Paid-In Capital	226,110
Land	20,000	Retained Earnings (Deficit)	(6,047)
		TOTAL (Shareholders' Equity)	231,953
TOTAL (Assets)	253,670	**TOTAL** (Liabilities and Shareholders' Equity)	253,670

Notice the net loss resulted in an equal amount of negative retained earnings. Remember, retained earnings equals net income only in the first period of operations. Also, a net loss results in a reduction to shareholders' equity. In this case, Will Knott Incorporated has a Retained Earnings deficit because it lost money in its first period of operations.

Will Knott General Journal - Closing Entries

Date September 30, 2004	Debit $	Credit $
Sales Revenue	9,420	
Income Summary		9,420
Explanation: To close sales revenue to income summary.		

Date September 30, 2004	Debit $	Credit $
Income Summary	1,400	
Advertising Expense		1,400
Explanation: To close advertising expense to income summary.		

Date September 30, 2004	Debit $	Credit $
Income Summary	2,600	
Maintenance Expense		2,600
Explanation: To close maintenance expense to income summary.		

Date September 30, 2004	Debit $	Credit $
Income Summary	1,000	
Organization Expense		1,000
Explanation: To close organization expense to income summary.		

Date September 30, 2004	Debit $	Credit $
Income Summary	6,000	
Wages Expense		6,000
Explanation: To close wages expense to income summary.		

Date September 30, 2004	Debit $	Credit $
Income Summary	875	
Miscellaneous Expense		875
Explanation: *To close miscellaneous expense to income summary.*		

Date September 30, 2004	Debit $	Credit $
Income Summary	650	
Utilities Expense		650
Explanation: *To close utilities expense to income summary.*		

Date September 30, 2004	Debit $	Credit $
Income Summary	200	
Insurance Expense		200
Explanation: *To close insurance expense to income summary.*		

Date September 30, 2004	Debit $	Credit $
Income Summary	67	
Interest Expense		67
Explanation: *To close interest expense to income summary.*		

Date September 30, 2004	Debit $	Credit $
Income Summary	1,800	
Office Supplies Expense		1,800
Explanation: *To close office supplies expense to income summary*		

Date September 30, 2004	Debit $	Credit $
Income Summary	875	
Depreciation Expense		875
Explanation: *To close depreciation expense to income summary*		

Date September 30, 2004	Debit $	Credit $
Retained Earnings	6,047	
Income Summary		6,047
Explanation: To close sales revenue to income summary		

Will Knott Incorporated
Post-Closing Trial Balance
As at September 30, 2004

Account	Debit $	Credit $
Cash	8,925	
Accounts Receivable	7,220	
Office Supplies	1,200	
Prepaid Insurance	2,200	
Equipment	15,000	
Accumulated Depreciation - Equipment		250
Building	200,000	
Accumulated Depreciation - Building		625
Land	20,000	
Accounts Payable		1,650
Bank Loan		20,000
Interest Payable		67
Share Capital		11,890
Additional Paid-In Capital		226,110
Retained Earnings	6,047	
TOTAL	**260,592**	**260,592**

Case Two

Havealot Limited

The balance sheet for Havealot Limited shows the following on
December 31, 2003:

Havealot Limited
Balance Sheet
As at December 31, 2003

Assets		Liabilities	
Cash	$10,000	Accounts payable	20,000
Account Receivable	30,450	Income Taxes Payable	5,430
Prepaid Insurance	4,800	Bank Loan	50,000
Prepaid Rent	24,000	**TOTAL** (Liabilities)	**75,430**
Machinery	500,000		
Less: Accumulated Depreciation	(22,820)	Shareholders' Equity	
		Authorized 1,000,000	120,000
		no-par common shares,	
		20,000 common shares issued	
		Retained Earnings	351,000
		TOTAL (Shareholders' Equity)	**471,000**
TOTAL (Assets)	**546,430**	**TOTAL** (Liabilities and Shareholders' Equity)	**546,430**

On January 31, 2004 the Trial Balance for Havealot Limited shows the following:

Havealot Limited
Trial Balance
As at January 31, 2004

Account	Debit $	Credit $
Cash	8,700	
Accounts Receivable	44,960	
Prepaid Insurance	4,800	
Prepaid Rent	24,000	
Machinery	500,000	
Accumulated Depreciation - Machinery		22,820
Accounts Payable		22,650
Income Taxes Payable		5,430
Bank Loan		50,000
Share Capital		120,000
Retained Earnings		351,000
Sales Revenue		19,500
Wages Expense	2,600	
Maintenance Expense	4,000	
Miscellaneous Expense	2,340	
TOTAL	**591,400**	**591,400**

The following additional information is available:

The December 31, 2003 balance sheet shows the amount of prepaid insurance and prepaid rent for the entire year, 2004.

The machinery is depreciated using the straight-line method. It has an expected life of 10 years with a salvage value of $50,000.

The bank loan is due in 2009. The next cash interest payment is due at the end of February, 2004. The interest rate is 6% per year.

Income taxes will be charged at a rate of 25% on any profit. Any taxes owed will be paid at the end of March, 2004.

Required:

Finish the accounting cycle for Havealot Limited for the month of January, 2004. You must:

Prepare the necessary adjusting entries and post them to the ledger.

Prepare an adjusted trial balance.

Prepare the income statement and balance sheet.

Prepare the closing entries and post them to the ledger.

Prepare a post-closing trial balance.

Use the space provided below.

Havealot Limited General Journal - Adjusting Entries

Date	Debit $	Credit $
Explanation:		

Computation:

Date	Debit $	Credit $
Explanation:		

Computation:

Date	Debit $	Credit $
Explanation:		

Computation:

Date		Debit $	Credit $
Explanation:			

Computation:

Date		Debit $	Credit $
Explanation:			

Computation:

Havealot Limited - General Ledger

Note: the trial balances have not been posted to the ledger.

Cash	Accounts Receivable	Prepaid Insurance

Prepaid Rent	Machinery	Accum. Dep'n. (mach.)

Accounts Payable	Interest Payable	Income Taxes Payable

Bank Loan

Share Capital

Retained Earnings

Sales Revenue

Wages Expense

Maintenance Expense   Miscellaneous Expense   Insurance Expense   Rent Expense

Depreciation Expense   Interest Expense   Income Tax Expense

Income Summary

Havealot Limited
Adjusted Trial Balance
As at _____

Account	Debit $	Credit $
TOTAL		

Havealot Limited
Income Statement
For the _____

Sales Revenue	
Expenses:	
Total Expenses	
Income Before Taxes	
Income Tax Expense - 25%	
Net Income for the month	

Havealot Limited
Balance Sheet
As at _____

Assets	Liabilities
	TOTAL (Liabilities)
	Shareholders' Equity
	TOTAL (Shareholders' Equity)
TOTAL (Assets)	**TOTAL** (Liabilities and Shareholders' Equity)

Havealot Limited General Journal - Closing Entries

Date	Debit $	Credit $
Explanation:		

Date	Debit $	Credit $
Explanation:		

Date	Debit $	Credit $
Explanation:		

Date	Debit $	Credit $
Explanation:		

Date	Debit $	Credit $
Explanation:		

Date	Debit $	Credit $
Explanation:		

Date	Debit $	Credit $
Explanation:		

Date	Debit $	Credit $
Explanation:		

Date	Debit $	Credit $
Explanation:		

Date	Debit $	Credit $
Explanation:		

Notes

_____

_____

_____

_____

_____

_____

_____

_____

_____

Havealot Limited
Post-Closing Trial Balance
As at _____

Account	Debit $	Credit $
TOTAL		

Solutions to Case Two

Havealot Limited General Journal - Adjusting Entries

Date *January 31, 2004*	Debit $	Credit $
Insurance Expense	400	
Prepaid Insurance		400
Explanation: To record insurance expense for the month of January.		

Computation: *$4,800 ÷ 12 months = $400 per month*

Date January 31, 2004	Debit $	Credit $
Rent Expense	2,000	
Prepaid Rent		2,000
Explanation: *To record rent expense for the month of January.*		

Computation: *$24,000 ÷ 12 months = $2000 per month*

Date January 31, 2004	Debit $	Credit $
Depreciation Expense	3,750	
Accumulated Depreciation - Machinery		3,750
Explanation: *To record depreciation expense for the month of January.*		

Computation: *($500,000 - $50,000) ÷ 10 years = $45,000 per year*
$45,000 ÷ 12 months = $3,750 per month

Date January 31, 2004	Debit $	Credit $
Interest Expense	250	
Interest Payable		250
Explanation: *To record interest expense for the month of January, incurred but not yet paid.*		

Computation: *$50,000 x 6% = $3,000 per year*
$3,000 ÷ 12 months = $250 per month

Date January 31, 2004	Debit $	Credit $
Income Tax Expense	1,040	
Income Taxes Payable		1,040
Explanation: *To record income tax expense for the month of January, incurred but not yet paid.*		

Computation: *$19,500 - $2,600 - $4,000 - $2,340 - $400 - $2,000 - $3,750 - $250 = $4,160*
in taxable income. $4,160 x 25% = $1,040

Havealot Limited - General Ledger

Note: shows all entries including closing.

Cash			Accounts Receivable			Prepaid Insurance	
8,700			44,960			4,800	400
						4,400	

Prepaid Rent			Machinery			Accum. Dep'n. (mach.)	
24,000	2,000		500,000				22,820
22,000							3,750
							26,570

Accounts Payable			Interest Payable			Income Taxes Payable	
	22,650			250			5,430
							1,040
							6,470

Bank Loan			Share Capital	
	50,000			120,000

Retained Earnings			Sales Revenue			Wages Expense	
	351,000		19,500	19,500		2,600	2,600
	3,120		0			0	
	354,120						

Maintenance Expense		Miscellaneous Expense		Insurance Expense		Rent Expense	
4,000	4,000	2,340	2,340	400	400	2,000	2,000
0		0		0		0	

Depreciation Expense	
3,750	3,750
0	

Interest Expense	
250	250
0	

Income Tax Expense	
1,040	1,040
0	

Income Summary	
	19,500
2,600	
4,000	
2,340	
400	
2,000	
3,750	
250	
1,040	
	3,120
3,120	
0	

Notes

_____
_____
_____
_____
_____
_____
_____
_____
_____
_____
_____
_____
_____
_____

Havealot Limited
Adjusted Trial Balance
As at January 31, 2004

Account	Debit $	Credit $
Cash	8,700	
Accounts Receivable	44,960	
Prepaid Insurance	4,400	
Prepaid Rent	22,000	
Machinery	500,000	
Accumulated Depreciation - Machinery		26,570
Accounts Payable		22,650
Interest Payable		250
Income Taxes Payable		6,470
Bank Loan		50,000
Share Capital		120,000
Retained Earnings		351,000
Sales Revenue		19,500
Wages Expense	2,600	
Maintenance Expense	4,000	
Miscellaneous Expense	2,340	
Insurance Expense	400	
Rent Expense	2,000	
Depreciation Expense	3,750	
Interest Expense	250	
Income Tax Expense	1,040	
TOTAL	**596,440**	**596,440**

Havealot Limited
Income Statement
For the month ended January 31, 2004

Sales Revenue		$19,500
Expenses:		
Wages	$2,600	
Maintenance	4,000	
Insurance	400	
Rent	2,000	
Depreciation	3,750	
Interest	250	
Miscellaneous	2,340	
Total Expenses		15,340
Income Before Taxes		4,160
Income Tax Expense - 25%		1,040
Net Income for the month		3,120

Havealot Limited
Balance Sheet
As at January 31, 2004

Assets		Liabilities	
Cash	$8,700	Accounts payable	22,650
Account Receivable	44,960	Interest Payable	250
Prepaid Insurance	4,400	Income Taxes Payable	6,470
Prepaid Rent	22,000	Bank Loan	50,000
Machinery	500,000	**TOTAL** (Liabilities)	79,370
Less: Accumulated Depreciation	(26,570)		
		Shareholders' Equity	
		Share Capital: authorized 1,000,000 no-par common shares, 20,000 common shares issued	120,000
		Retained Earnings	354,120
		TOTAL (Shareholders' Equity)	474,120
TOTAL (Assets)	553,490	**TOTAL** (Liabilities and Shareholders' Equity)	553,490

Havealot Limited General Journal - Closing Entries

Date January 31, 2004	Debit $	Credit $
Sales Revenue	19,500	
Income Summary		19,500
Explanation: To close sales revenue to income summary		

Date January 31, 2004	Debit $	Credit $
Income Summary	2,600	
Wages Expense		2,600
Explanation: To close wages expense to income summary		

Date January 31, 2004	Debit $	Credit $
Income Summary	4,000	
Maintenance Expense		4,000
Explanation: To close maintenance expense to income summary		

Date January 31, 2004	Debit $	Credit $
Income Summary	2,340	
Miscellaneous Expense		2,340
Explanation: To close miscellaneous expense to income summary		

Date January 31, 2004	Debit $	Credit $
Income Summary	400	
Insurance Expense		400
Explanation: To close insurance expense to income summary		

Date January 31, 2004	Debit $	Credit $
Income Summary	2,000	
Rent Expense		2,000
Explanation: To close rent expense to income summary		

Date January 31, 2004	Debit $	Credit $
Income Summary	3,750	
Depreciation Expense		3,750
Explanation: To close depreciation expense to income summary		

Date January 31, 2004	Debit $	Credit $
Income Summary	250	
Interest Expense		250
Explanation: To close interest expense to income summary		

Date January 31, 2004	Debit $	Credit $
Income Summary	1,040	
Income Tax Expense		1,040
Explanation: To close income tax expense to income summary		

Date January 31, 2004	Debit $	Credit $
Income Summary	3,120	
Retained Earnings		3,120
Explanation: To close income summary to retained earnings		

Notes

_____
_____
_____
_____
_____
_____
_____
_____
_____

Havealot Limited
Post-Closing Trial Balance
As at January 31, 2004

Account	Debit $	Credit $
Cash	8,700	
Accounts Receivable	44,960	
Prepaid Insurance	4,400	
Prepaid Rent	22,000	
Machinery	500,000	
Accumulated Depreciation - Machinery		26,570
Accounts Payable		22,650
Interest Payable		250
Income Taxes Payable		6,470
Bank Loan		50,000
Share Capital		120,000
Retained Earnings		354,120
TOTAL	580,060	580,060

Notes

_____
_____
_____
_____
_____
_____
_____
_____
_____
_____
_____
_____

Notes

Accounting for Corporations

Chapter Four - Distributing Dividends

The Reason for This Chapter

In this chapter we account for payments to shareholders. We call these payments dividends. While we consider them to be a reward for ownership, they are not a legal obligation. Normally, dividends refer to a cash payment. However, stock dividends are sometimes given. We examine both types of dividends in this Chapter.

In Chapter Four we complete the accounting cycle. To do so, we must revisit the closing entries needed at the end of the accounting period. As we shall see, dividend declarations are closed to Retained Earnings.

What Do You Already Know?

In this section of the chapter we ask you to complete a pre-test. It will get you thinking about what you already know about accounting. It will also serve as a link between what you learned in Chapters One and Two, and what you are about to learn in Chapter Four. After completing the pre-test, check your answers against the ones provided.

Question One

Allsorts Incorporated has just made a record profit of $233,590. The company's retained earnings account shows a balance of $870,300. Today, March 31, 2004 the company is closing their books for the year. The final journal entry to close the income summary account is missing. Use the space provided to prepare this entry. What is the retained earnings balance on the March 31, 2004 balance sheet?

Allsorts Incorporated - General Journal

Date	Debit $	Credit $
Explanation:		

Retained Earnings balance on March 31, 2004:

_____

Question Two

Ping and Peter are equal partners in their business "The Pinter Partnership". On July 5, 2004, Peter encounters a personal financial problem and needs $5,000 cash immediately. He withdraws money from the business. Record the journal entry for this transaction. What will happen to the partners' equity as a result of this transaction?

Pinter Partnership - General Journal

Date	Debit $	Credit $
Explanation:		

Partners' equity:

_____
_____
_____
_____
_____

Answer to Question One

Allsorts Incorporated - General Journal

Date March 31, 2004	Debit $	Credit $
Income Summary	233,590	
Retained Earnings		233,590
Explanation: *To close Income Summary to Retained Earnings*		

Retained Earnings balance on March 31, 2004: $870,300 + $233,590 = $1,103,890

Answer to Question Two

Pinter Partnership - General Journal

Date July 5, 2004	Debit $	Credit $
Withdrawals, Peter	5,000	
Cash		5,000
Explanation: *To record Peter's withdrawal of cash from his business.*		

Partners' equity: will decrease by $5,000, the amount of cash withdrawn from the business. The Statement of Partners' Capital should account for the withdrawal under Peter's name. Thus, Peter's Capital account will be $5,000 less and the total equity in the business will also be $5,000 less.

How This Chapter Relates to Other Chapters in This Book

Chapter One examined share issuance and provided an introduction to the Shareholders' Equity account, Share Capital. Chapter Two presented a second equity account, Retained Earnings. In this chapter we explore a related process, dividend payments.

The Retained Earnings account shows how the corporation accumulates profits. However, from time to time there may be withdrawals from this account. Such an action reflects money given to the owners. We refer to this transaction as a dividend distribution.

Accounting for dividends is not unlike accounting for owner's withdrawals. However, the nature and process is more complex. We examine all these topics in this chapter.

What Are the Topics in This Chapter?

As you know, the main reporting difference (between Corporations and the other forms of business can be found in the Equity Section of the balance sheet. In keeping with this theme, we now look at distributions to owners - the dividend payment. This requires that we examine the nature of these payments, the process of paying and their accounting treatment. A related topic is covered briefly - stock dividends.

Topics Covered in Chapter Four	Level of Importance
What Are Dividends?	
Definition	**
Like Withdrawals	**
Unlike Withdrawals	***
Should Dividends Be Paid?	
View of Shareholders	**
View of Management	**
Distribution versus Retention	***
Important Dividend Dates	
Declaration Date	***
Record Date	**
Payment Date	**
The Quarterly Tradition	**
Journal Entries	
Immediate Payment	***
Deferred Payment	***
Closing the Books	
The Link to Profits	***
Closing Journal Entries	???
About Stock Dividends	
A Reason For	**
A Reason Against	**
Journal Entries - Stock Dividends	
No-Par value Stock Dividends	**
Par-Value Stock Dividends	**

Legend

*   indicates a low level of importance
**   indicates a medium level of importance
***   indicates a high level of importance

What Are Dividends?

Definition

When the corporation makes a profit, part of it may be distributed to shareholders. We refer to the portion of net income distributed to shareholders as a dividend distribution. While shareholders own the entire net income, dividends result when some of that net income is actually distributed to shareholders. A dividend results in less retained earnings.

Like Withdrawals

Just like sole proprietorships and partnerships, a dividend payment represents the withdrawal of equity by owners of the corporation. Similar to withdrawals, we view a dividend payment as a reward of ownership. The owners have the right to withdraw money from the business. When this happens, their investment in the business is reduced. We account for this by decreasing the value of equity.

Unlike Withdrawals

Unlike sole proprietorships and partnerships, the dividend payment is not a decision of the owners. Management runs the corporation - not the shareholders. Management reports to the board of directors. Ultimately, this board must approve all decisions because they report to shareholders. Thus, the company's board of directors determine both the timing and size of any dividend payments. In a sole proprietorship or partnership, the owners run the business. It is they who decide both the size and timing of any withdrawals.

Should Dividends Be Paid?

So when does the corporation pay dividends? How much is paid? These are not simple questions to answer. However, exploring different viewpoints provides some insight into when and why a dividend payment is made.

View of Shareholders

When the corporation does well, the owners should benefit. One way to reward shareholders is through the distribution of a dividend payment. However, dividend payments reduce the shareholders' investment in the business. The total amount of equity will decline. In addition, there is an offsetting reduction in assets. Reasons may exist that make this undesirable. So, the board of directors will have the final say.

Does this lack of control hurt shareholders? Not necessarily. Remember, for public corporations, the shareholders are free to sell all, or a portion of their shares at any time. Thus, if the corporation does well but decides not to make a dividend payment, the shareholders can still generate their own reward. How? By selling shares. If the business thrives, the stock price should rise. Shareholders may realize a reward by selling their shares at a higher price.

For shareholders in a private corporation, the dividend question is more complicated. Since it is harder for them to sell their shares at any time, they may depend on receiving dividend payments. When the dividend payment is expected, more pressure is placed on management to make it happen.

View of Management

Management operates the business on a day-to-day basis. It is their job to ensure the value of the business increases over time. How is this achieved? By making decisions that result in increased profits.

Commonly, higher profits result from investing in new assets. As long as the benefits are greater than the costs of doing so, net income should rise. Thus, management may constantly need money to make new investments.

A dividend payment is a distribution of money out of the firm. If management needs money to make new investments, they may want to restrict or eliminate the dividend payment.

Distribution versus Retention

The decision of when and how much to pay in dividends is mainly a result of the corporation's investment opportunities. When there are a lot of great opportunities for the business to grow, it makes good sense to put any earnings back into the business. Retaining earnings increases equity. It makes more money available for expansion. Paying dividends reduces the amount of money available for expansion.

When there are no investment opportunities in the foreseeable future, net income should be distributed to owners. After all, net income is owned by the shareholders. If management can not make a profitable investment with it, they should give it back to the owners. They can do so by making a dividend payment.

However, even when no investment opportunities exist, the dividend payment may still be less than net income. Why? Because net income does not necessarily equal cash flow. Remember, under the accrual system of accounting our objective is to report earnings, not cash. At the end of the accounting period it is generally true that not all revenues have been collected as cash, nor have all expenses been paid with cash. The balance sheet reflects these accounts as receivables and payables. Also, the depreciation charge on the income statement is not paid to anyone - it is a non-cash expense. In addition to investment opportunities, the dividend payment is also constrained by the amount of available cash.

Shareholders are not usually aware of either the business opportunities available to the company or the amount of available cash. It is the job of management to have such information. Shareholders must rely on the board of directors to make the right dividend decision.

When the result of operating the business is a net loss, there is really no decision to make regarding dividend payments. Generally, there should be no dividend distribution when a company incurs a loss. However, because dividend payments are made regularly, shareholders come to expect them. Pressure exists for management to maintain dividend payments each period.

Because the decision to make a dividend payment is so complex we conclude this discussion here. We expect that you appreciate the dilemma management faces in this regard. We continue our study by examining the process behind actually making the payment.

Important Dividend Dates

In order to account for dividend payments we must first understand the process of how they come into being. We will examine three important dates: the declaration, record and payment dates.

Declaration Date

Once management proposes the dividend decision, the board of directors meet to approve it. Once approved, they publicly declare the corporation's intention to make a dividend payment. This is usually done by newspaper advertisement, and is called the declaration date.

This important date represents a legal liability for the corporation. Unlike interest payments on loans, dividends are not a legal right of shareholders unless they have been declared by the board of directors. Once declared, the liability is created.

Usually, the dividend is not actually paid on the declaration date. First, the corporation must determine to whom the payments should be made. It does so by compiling a list of shareholders. We examine the record date, next.

Record Date

When the dividend is declared, the record date is announced. All shareholders on record as of that date will receive the dividend payment. Establishing the record date is necessary because shareholders may change each day. Every time a stock trades, the ownership structure changes. For public corporations, this may happen daily.

So, the record date is a cut-off date to establish who is deemed an owner and will receive the payment. It is a specific calendar date that follows the declaration date.

Payment Date

The dividend payment is not actually made until the payment date. Generally, this date occurs within thirty days of the record date. Once the complete list of shareholders - those on record - has been compiled, the dividend checks are mailed. On the payment date the cash account is reduced by the dollar amount of the dividend payment.

The Quarterly Tradition

Most public corporations provide financial reports on a quarterly basis. They release the financial statements every three months to offer investors timely information about the company's performance.

Following with this tradition, most public corporations declare a dividend payment on a quarterly basis. While not required to do so, the practice is widely followed. Thus, shareholders come to expect some announcement regarding dividend payments every three months. When a corporation fails to make the quarterly dividend announcement, the public tends to adopt the view that something is wrong. Because of this, management usually makes every effort to announce a quarterly dividend payment.

You should keep in mind that a corporation may elect to make a dividend payment whenever the board of directors believes it is appropriate to do so.

Now You Try It

Exercise One

On July 1, 2004, the Board of Directors of Kellwing Inc. met to review the company's second quarter performance. As part of its duties, the Board approved a proposed dividend payment of $0.50 per common share.

Following the Board meeting, the company placed an advertisement in the National Paper. It announced its intention to make a dividend payment to shareholders on record as of August 1, 2004.

What is the declaration date, record date and payment date of the $0.50 per share dividend for Kellwing Inc.? Justify your answer.

_____

_____

_____

_____

_____

_____

Answers

Answer to Exercise One

Declaration Date: July 1, 2004. This is the date the Board met and publicly declared a dividend payment would be made.

Record Date: August 1, 2004. This date establishes to whom the dividends will be paid. Anyone purchasing shares of Kellwing Inc. on or before this date will be deemed a holder of record and will receive the dividend payment.

Payment Date: unknown. The information provided does not state when the dividend checks will be mailed.

Journal Entries

Immediate Payment

When the corporation decides to make an immediate dividend payment, two accounts are affected: cash and retained earnings. While this is not the usual procedure, it may happen from time to time. Try Exercise Two to practice the journal entries for a cash dividend payment.

Now You Try It

Exercise Two

On May 15, 2004, Masters Limited has approved an immediate cash dividend of $0.25 per common share. According to its charter the company is authorized to issue 1,000,000 common shares; 350,000 common shares are actually outstanding as at May 15, 2004. Record the journal entry for the payment of this dividend.

Masters Limited - General Journal

Date	Debit $	Credit $
Explanation:		

Computation:

Answers

Answer to Exercise Two

Masters Limited - General Journal

Date May 15, 2004	Debit $	Credit $
Retained Earnings	87,500	
Cash		87,500
Explanation: *To record a cash dividend payment of $0.25 per common share on 350,000 outstanding shares.*		

Computation: *$0.25 x 350,000 = $87,500*

Note: Dividends are paid on outstanding (not on authorized) shares. Since only 350,000 of the authorized shares have been distributed, the $0.25 dividend payment must be made on these shares only.

Deferred Payment

The natural dividend payment process follows the sequence: declaration date, record date and finally payment date. Since the dividend payment becomes a legal liability on the date it is declared, we must account for it then. However, as it is not paid out on that date we record the declaration as a deferral. By crediting the account "Dividends Payable". A credit to the cash account occurs when the actual payment takes place. Try Exercise Three to practice deferred dividend payments.

Now You Try It

Exercise Three

On March 31, 2004, Tippers Incorporated declared its intention to pay a $0.85 dividend per common share to all holders of record as at April 30, 2004. The dividend checks will be mailed 30 days after the record date. According to its charter the company is authorized to issue 500,000 common shares; as at March 31, 2004, 150,000 common shares are actually outstanding. It is not expected that any additional shares will be issued before May 30, 2004. Record the necessary journal entries.

Tippers Incorporated - General Journal

Date	Debit $	Credit $
Explanation:		

Computation:

Date	Debit $	Credit $
Explanation:		

Answers

Answer to Exercise Three

Tippers Incorporated - General Journal

Date March 31, 2004	Debit $	Credit $
Retained Earnings	127,500	
Dividends Payable		127,500
Explanation: *To record a declared dividend payment of $0.85 per common share on 150,000 outstanding shares.*		

Computation: *$0.85 x 150,000 = $127,500*

Date May 30, 2004*	Debit $	Credit $
Dividends Payable	127,500	
Cash		127,500
Explanation: *To record the payment of the declared dividend.*		

*Note: the payment date is 30 days after the April 30, 2004 record date.

Closing the Books

The Link to Profits

Why do we "pay" dividends from retained earnings? Recall, dividends represent a reward of ownership. When the business does well, management may elect to distribute some wealth back to the shareholders. Since the dividend decision is based largely upon the performance of the corporation, the declaration of a dividend reduces retained earnings. In this way we account for the promise to give some equity back to shareholders, because the business operated at a profit.

It is important to note that whenever we say dividends are "paid" from retained earnings we are simply emphasizing the point that all dividends reduce the Retained Earnings account. Only the actual *payment* of a cash dividend reduces the cash account. Furthermore, a large Retained Earnings account balance does not mean a company has sufficient cash to make a dividend payment.

The dividend declaration represents a promise to pay. We report it as a deferred liability because the corporation has promised to pay the dividend amount in the future. Once the cash payment is actually made, we reduce that asset account and the deferred liability account.

The diagram below demonstrates the link between net income, retained earnings and dividends.

The Link to Profits

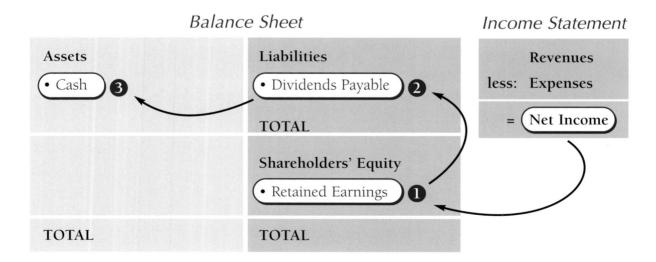

1 Net income is credited to Retained Earnings

2 Retained Earnings are debited by Dividends Payable

3 Dividends payable are paid with cash

Closing Journal Entries

The Income Summary account is not affected by dividend declarations or the actual dividend payments. By crediting Net Income to Retained Earnings, the temporary account Income Summary is closed. The dividend declaration reduces Retained Earnings directly (we debit Retained Earnings). There is a simultaneous credit to Dividends Payable when the payment is deferred or Cash, if payment is immediate.

Try Exercise Four to practice closing the books when a dividend is declared.

Now You Try It

Exercise Four

Excerpts from the most recent Income Statement for Brass Boys Corporation show the following:

Brass Boys Corporation
Income Statement
For the three months ending September 30, 2004

Revenues	$64,850
Expenses	(35,870)
Net Income	$28,980

In addition, the board declared a dividend of $0.45 per common share on September 30, 2004 payable to all holders of record as at October 31, 2004. The dividend payment will be issued on November 15, 2004. There are 10,000 common shares outstanding.

Use the space provided to prepare the closing journal entries and the entries needed to record the dividend transaction.

Brass Boys Corporation - General Journal

Date	Debit $	Credit $
Explanation:		

Date	Debit $	Credit $
Explanation:		

Date	Debit $	Credit $
Explanation:		

Computation:

Date	Debit $	Credit $
Explanation:		

Computation:

Date	Debit $	Credit $
Explanation:		

Answers

Answer to Exercise Four

Brass Boys Corporation - General Journal

Date September 30, 2004	Debit $	Credit $
Revenues	64,850	
Income Summary		64,850
Explanation: *To close revenues to income summary.*		

Date September 30, 2004	Debit $	Credit $
Income Summary	35,870	
Expenses		35,870
Explanation: *To close expenses to income summary.*		

Date September 30, 2004	Debit $	Credit $
Income Summary	28,980	
Retained Earnings		28,980
Explanation: *To close income summary to retained earnings.*		

Computation: $64,850 - $35,870 = $28,980

Date September 30, 2004	Debit $	Credit $
Retained Earnings	4,500	
Dividends Payable		4,500
Explanation: *To record the declaration of a dividend of $0.45 per common share on 10,000 outstanding shares.*		

Computation: $0.45 x 10,000 = $4,500

Date November 15, 2004	Debit $	Credit $
Dividends Payable	4,500	
Cash		4,500
Explanation: To record the payment of the declared dividend.		

About Stock Dividends

Instead of making a cash dividend payment, corporations may issue stocks in lieu of cash. That is, instead of mailing dividend checks, the company gives shareholders additional stocks. The number of additional shares will carry the same dollar value as the dividend payment.

A Reason For

Why offer stocks instead of cash? While many reasons may exist, the consequence of giving stock dividends is that the company will conserve cash. When companies are short of cash but wish to reward shareholders, they may offer a stock dividend in place of a cash dividend. This may be justified when the corporation has exciting investment prospects.

Usually, the corporation distributes stock dividends on a pro-rata basis. That is, the number of stock dividends received by any shareholder is based on the percentage of shares currently owned.

Try Exercise Five to practice computing pro-rata stock dividends.

Now You Try It

Exercise Five

Shirley Chu owns 12,000 common shares of Cashnot Corporation. On January 15, 2004 the company announces its intention to distribute a 10% stock dividend to all shareholders. On that date 100,000 common shares of Cashnot are outstanding. How many shares will Shirley receive as a stock dividend? Use the following table to guide you:

Outstanding Shares	X stock dividend percentage	= number of additional shares issued as stock dividend	X percentage owned by shareholder	= number of additional shares issued to shareholder

Answers

Answer to Exercise Five

First we compute the percentage ownership of Shirley Chu:

12,000 ÷ 100,000 = 0.12 or 12%.

Therefore the number of shares issued to Shirley as a stock dividend on a pro-rata basis will be:

Outstanding Shares	X stock dividend percentage	= number of additional shares issued as stock dividend	X percentage owned by shareholder	= number of additional shares issued to shareholder
100,000	X 10%	= 10,000 shares	X 12%	= 1,200 shares

A Reason Against

From the perspective of shareholders, a stock dividend is not the same thing as cash. Cash is an asset that can be used by the investor to purchase goods and services. It has a stable value.

A stock dividend is not a readily negotiable instrument. Investors must convert stocks into cash before they can use the money. The conversion takes place at an uncertain price, as most stocks trade daily. Thus, if the performance of the corporation is poor, the value of the stock and the stock dividend declines.

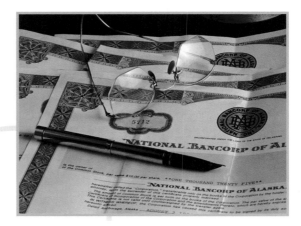

Because a cash shortage may indicate poor performance, shareholders should not readily accept a stock dividend in lieu of a cash payment. Clearly, cash in hand is more valuable than share certificates that have an uncertain value.

The arguments for and against stock dividends can be numerous. Shareholders should concern themselves with the reasons behind the stock dividend. Professionals like accountants and financial analysts often perform this function on behalf of shareholders.

Journal Entries - Stock Dividends

No-Par Value Stock Dividends

The declaration of a dividend always reduces Retained Earnings. This is true whether it is a cash or stock dividend. However, when a stock dividend is declared no liability is created. The corporation has simply committed to issue more shares. They have not promised to pay out a cash asset.

In the case of a stock dividend the declaration and issue dates are often the same day. We will assume so in this book.

The stock dividend does not really change the value of anything. The additional issued shares increase the Share Capital account.

However, the issue reduces Retained Earnings. Therefore we increase one equity account and decrease another, by exactly the same dollar amount.

One consequence of a stock dividend is the reduction of the value per share. While the dollar value of shareholders' equity does not change, the number of shares outstanding will increase. Because there are more shares outstanding and the value of equity has not changed, the value per share must decline.

We record a stock dividend by using the market price of the shares on the date the dividend is declared. We debit Retained Earnings by the total amount of the stock dividend, and credit Share Capital account, by the same amount. Try Exercise Six to practice the journal entries for stock dividends.

Now You Try It

Exercise Six

Cashnot Corporation has several exciting investment projects to consider. Unfortunately, it suffers from a temporary cash shortage. On January 15, 2004 the company announces its intention to immediately issue a 10% stock dividend to all shareholders of record on January 15, 2004. On that date 100,000 no-par common shares are outstanding, and the market price per share is $20. Prepare the journal entry needed to record the stock dividend.

Cashnot Corporation - General Journal

Date	Debit $	Credit $
Explanation:		

Computation:

Answers

Answer to Exercise Six

Cashnot Corporation - General Journal

Date January, 2004	Debit $	Credit $
Retained Earnings	200,000	
Share Capital		200,000
Explanation: To record the issue of 10,000 no-par common shares at $20 each as a stock dividend.		

Computation: $20 x 100,000 x 10% = $200,000 or 10,000 x $20 = $200,000

You should note that no assets are affected by the issuance of a stock dividend. We used the market price per share to transfer $200,000 out of Retained Earnings into the Share Capital account.

Par-Value Stock Dividends

We follow the same basic process for issuing stock dividends regardless of whether or not the shares have a par-value. Thus, the overall effect is the same. However, par-value shares require the use of the Additional Paid-In Capital account. We must use it to record the stock dividend amount in excess of the par-value. That is, when the market price per share exceeds the par value, we record the excess as Additional Paid-In Capital. Try Exercise Seven to prepare journal entries for stock dividends on par-value shares.

Now You Try It

Exercise Seven

Cashalot Corporation has several exciting investment projects to consider. Instead of depleting its cash account, the Board decides to issue a stock dividend. On February 15, 2004 the company announces its intention to immediately issue a 10% stock dividend to all shareholders of record on February 15, 2004. On that date 100,000 $2 par-value common shares are outstanding, and the market price per share is $20. Prepare the journal entry needed to record the stock dividend.

Cashalot Corporation - General Journal

Date	Debit $	Credit $
Explanation:		

Computation:

Answers

Answer to Exercise Seven

Cashalot Corporation - General Journal

Date February 15, 2004	Debit $	Credit $
Retained Earnings	200,000	
Share Capital		20,000
Additional Paid-In Capital		180,000
Explanation: To record the issue of 10,000 common shares at $20 each as a stock dividend.		

Computation: 100,000 x 10% = 10,000 <u>shares</u>

10,000 x $2   = $ 20,000

10,000 x ($20 - $2) = $180,000

TOTAL   <u>$200,000</u>

Again, notice no assets are affected by the issuance of a stock dividend. We used the market price per share to transfer $200,000 out of Retained Earnings. We transfer it into the Share Capital account at its par of $2 per share. The excess ($18 per share) is recorded as Additional Paid-In Capital.

What You Have Learned in This Chapter

Chapter Four described the justification, process and accounting for dividend distributions. Two types of dividend payments were examined: Cash dividends and Stock dividends. Emphasis was given to the cash dividend, as it is the more valuable of the two.

By defining important dividend dates we aided your understanding of the process followed in paying dividends. Examination of the difference between withdrawals and dividend payments assisted your comprehension of when and why dividend payments are made.

Chapter Four also discussed the journal entries for both cash and stock dividends. The link between profits and dividend declarations and payments was provided. This demonstration supported the accounting process of reducing Retained Earnings whenever dividends are declared.

Important Terms in This Chapter

Accrual system: revenues are recorded when they are earned, not necessarily only when the cash is received. Similarly, expenses are recorded when they are incurred, not necessarily only when cash is disbursed. In other words, the objective of the accrual approach is to report earnings, not cash.

Declaration date: the date the Board of Directors announces the company's intention to make a dividend payment. The liability for the dividend is created on this date.

Dividends: the portion of net income distributed to shareholders as a reward of ownership. Dividends are usually paid in cash, but stock dividends also exist.

No-Par Stock Dividends: the dollar value of the stock dividend is transferred from Retained Earnings into Share Capital. The market price per share as at the declaration date is used to calculate the value of the transfer.

Par-Value Stock Dividends: the dollar value of the stock dividend is transferred from Retained Earnings into Share Capital (up to par) and Additional Paid-in Capital (amount in excess of par). The market price per share as at the declaration date is used to calculate the value of the transfer.

Payment date: the date the dividend is actually paid. This is usually the same day that the dividend checks are mailed, or deposited directly into the bank account of the recipient. On this date the cash account is reduced by the dollar amount of the dividend payment.

Pro-rata: the number of stocks a shareholder receives in a stock dividend distribution is based on the percentage of shares owned by the shareholder on the record date.

Quarterly tradition: for public corporations dividends are usually declared and paid every three months.

Record date: a cut-off date to establish who is deemed an owner and will therefore receive the dividend. It is a particular calendar date, it follows the declaration date.

Stock Dividend: the corporation issues additional stocks instead of cash as a dividend.

Withdrawals: a reduction in the equity of the business at the discretion of the owner (sole proprietor or partner). Usually takes the form of a cash payment.

Should You Move on to the Next Chapter?

Now it's time to check and see how comfortable you are with your new knowledge. Perform the Self-Test to verify whether you should move on, or go back and review the information contained in this chapter.

Self-Test for Chapter Four

Question One

What are the effects of a cash dividend on the assets and shareholders' equity of the company that declares the dividend?

_____

_____

_____

_____

_____

_____

Question Two

From the list of terms, select one term that is most closely associated with one descriptive phrase or statement that follows. Place the letter for that term in the space provided.

      A. common shares

      B. additional paid-in capital

      C. certificate of incorporation

      D. par value

      E. stock dividends

      F. declaration date

1. An issue of an additional number of shares to shareholders in proportion to their existing holdings without any additional contribution from them. _____

2. The voting class of share that also has a claim on any earnings. _____

3. A value per share specified in the certificate of incorporation. _____

4. The agreement between the firm and the jurisdiction in which the business is incorporated. _____

5. The account title used to designate capital contributed by owners in excess of par value. _____

6. The date the corporation announces its intention to make a dividend payment. _____

Question Three

For each statement, determine whether it is true or false by placing the word True or False after each statement. Briefly explain why the statement is true or false.

1. The corporate form of business provides the owner, or shareholder, with unlimited liability.

   _____
   _____
   _____
   _____

2. It is difficult to raise large amounts of money for corporations because so many shares of relatively small value must be sold.

   _____
   _____
   _____
   _____

3. Common shareholders have a claim to the corporation's net income.

   _____
   _____
   _____
   _____

4. Corporations generally pay dividends out of the earnings.

   _____
   _____
   _____
   _____

5. Par-value and no-par value shares have basically the same effect on shareholders' equity.

   _____
   _____
   _____
   _____

6. At the end of the accounting period, a well-managed firm will have cash equal to the amount of net income.

_____

_____

_____

_____

7. For most companies, dividend declarations are determined by shareholders at their annual meeting.

_____

_____

_____

_____

8. In most cases, corporations pay out dividends equal to net income.

_____

_____

_____

_____

9. Shareholders place the same value on a stock dividend as a cash dividend.

_____

_____

_____

_____

10. When a stock dividend is distributed, the par value of each share is reduced.

_____

_____

_____

_____

Question Four

The board of directors of Paters Limited declared a dividend of $0.25 per common share on March 31, 2004, payable to all holders of record at April 30, 2004. The dividend payment will be made on May 15, 2004. On March 31, 2004 and April 30, 2004 there are 10,000 common shares outstanding, each with a par value of $1.

Use the space provided below to prepare the journal entries needed to record the dividend transaction.

Paters Limited - General Journal

Date	Debit $	Credit $
Explanation:		

Computation:

Date	Debit $	Credit $
Explanation:		

Answers to Self-Test for Chapter Four

Answer to Question One

A cash dividend is "paid" from Retained Earnings. Thus, the dividend should only be declared if there is both sufficient cash AND retained earnings. The declaration of a dividend establishes an immediate liability. The result is a reduction to shareholders' equity because the Retained Earnings account is reduced by the amount of the dividend. Usually the liability account, Dividends Payable, reflects the amount of the dividend declared. The asset account, Cash, is reduced when the cash dividend is actually paid.

Answer to Question Two

1. An issue of an additional number of shares to shareholders in proportion to their existing holdings without any additional contribution from them. *E - stock dividends.*

2. The voting class of share that also has a claim on any earnings. *A - common shares.*

3. A value per share specified in the certificate of incorporation. *D - par value.*

4. The agreement between the firm and the jurisdiction in which the business is incorporated. *C - certificate of incorporation.*

5. The account title used to designate capital contributed by owners in excess of par value. *B - additional paid-in capital.*

6. The date the corporation announces its intention to make a dividend payment. *F -declaration date.*

Answer to Question Three

1. The corporate form of business provides the owner, or shareholder, with unlimited liability. *False. The shareholder enjoys limited liability.*

2. It is difficult to raise large amounts of money for corporations because so many shares of relatively small value must be sold. *False. Corporations are able to raise large amounts of money because their shares may be offered for sale to the public at large.*

3. Common shareholders have a claim to the corporation's net income. *True. Net income represents the earnings left-over once everyone else has been paid. Thus, shareholders own net income.*

4. Corporations generally pay dividends out of the earnings. *True. Dividends represent a reward to shareholders when the business does well.*

5. Par-value and no-par value shares have basically the same effect on shareholders' equity. *True. The total effect is the same. Par-value shares reflect the same total amount of equity (as if no-par value shares were used) but use both the share capital and additional paid-in capital accounts to do so.*

6. At the end of the accounting period, a well-managed firm will have cash equal to the amount of net income. *False. Net income is generally not equal to cash because of the existence of payables, receivables and non-cash charges like depreciation.*

7. For most companies, dividend declarations are determined by shareholders at their annual meeting. *False. Management proposes dividend declarations and the board of directors is responsible for authorizing the dividend. Usually this takes place quarterly for large, public corporations.*

8. In most cases, corporations pay out dividends equal to net income. *False. Dividends are usually linked to future investment opportunities. Also, since net income is not cash, the dividend payment is generally different (usually less).*

9. Shareholders place the same value on a stock dividend as a cash dividend. *False. Cash is more valuable because it is the most liquid of assets and can be used anywhere.*

10. When a stock dividend is distributed, the par value of each share is reduced. *False. Par value is usually never changed because it is fixed in the certificate of incorporation.*

Answer to Question Four

Paters Limited - General Journal

Date March 31, 2004	Debit $	Credit $
Retained Earnings	2,500	
Dividends Payable		2,500
Explanation: To record a declared dividend payment of $0.25 per common share on 10,000 outstanding shares.		

Computation: $0.25 x 10,000 = $2,500

Date May 15, 2004	Debit $	Credit $
Dividends Payable	2,500	
Cash		2,500
Explanation: To record the dividend payment of $0.25 per common share on 10,000 outstanding shares.		

Note: Par value is not affected by the dividend payment. The record date is used to determine to whom the actual dividend checks will be mailed.

Practice Problems for Chapter Four

Question One

Record the following entries in the general journal of Ameri-Eng Corporation. Use the space provided below:

January 13, 2003. Issued 1,000 common shares for $15 cash per share. The common shares show a par value of $10 per share.

January 30, 2003. Issued a 10 percent stock dividend on the common shares. At the time of issue there were 100,000 shares outstanding and each share had a market value of $16.

February 28, 2003. Declared a cash dividend totaling $220,000 to common shareholders.

March 31, 2003. Closed the income summary balance of $300,000 to retained earnings.

March 31, 2003. Paid the dividend declared on February 28, 2003.

Ameri-Eng Corporation - General Journal

Date				Debit $	Credit $
Explanation:					

Computation:

Date				Debit $	Credit $
Explanation:					

Computation:

Date				Debit $	Credit $
Explanation:					

Computation:

Date		Debit $	Credit $
Explanation:			

Date		Debit $	Credit $
Explanation:			

Question Two

The following table shows the shareholders' equity section of the balance sheet for Lowlie Incorporated at the end of 2002 and 2003. On May 25, 2003, Lowlie Incorporated issued new shares for $40 per share. Its revenues for 2003 were $90,100 net income was $10,100.

Lowlie Incorporated Balance Sheet
Shareholders' Equity

Shareholders' Equity	Dec. 31, 2003	Dec. 31, 2002
Share Capital ($5 par value per common share)	5,500	5,000
Additional Paid-In Capital	33,500	30,000
Retained Earnings	66,450	59,100
Total Shareholders' Equity	$105,450	$94,100

Reconstruct all of the transactions involving shareholders' equity accounts for 2003, including closing entries. Show the journal entries for those transactions. Use the following spaces provided:

Lowlie Incorporated - General Journal

Date		Debit $	Credit $
Explanation:			

Computation:

Date		Debit $	Credit $
Explanation:			

Date		Debit $	Credit $
Explanation:			

Computation:

Date		Debit $	Credit $
Explanation:			

Date	Debit $	Credit $
Explanation:		

Computation:

Question Three

On December 31, 2003, the shareholders' equity section of the balance sheet for Shellee Corporation reflects the following:

Share Capital, no par, 20,000 common shares
outstanding $115,000

Retained Earnings 103,000

On February 1, 2004, the Board of Directors declared and issued a 20% common stock dividend. The market value per share on that date was $15.

Required:

1. Provide the journal entry needed to record the stock dividend.

2. Calculate the average book value per share immediately before and after the stock dividend.

3. Explain why the average book value per share has changed. Refer to the effects of this stock dividend on the assets, liabilities and shareholders' equity of Shellee Corporation.

Use the space provided to answer each question:

Requirement One:

Shellee Corporation - General Journal

Date		Debit $	Credit $
Explanation:			

Computation:

Requirement Two:

Use the formula: total shareholders' equity ÷ # of shares = average book value per share:

Shareholders' Equity before stock dividend	# of shares before stock dividend	Average book value before stock dividend

Shareholders' Equity after stock dividend	# of shares after stock dividend	Average book value after stock dividend

Requirement Three:

_____

_____

_____

_____

_____

_____

Solutions to Practice Problems for Chapter Four

Solution to Question One

Ameri-Eng Corporation - General Journal

Date January 13, 2003	Debit $	Credit $
Cash	15,000	
Share Capital		10,000
Additional Paid-In Capital		5,000
Explanation: *To record the issue of 1,000 $10 par value shares at $15 each.*		

Computation: 1,000 x $10 = $10,000
1,000 x ($15 - $10) = $5,000
$10,000 + $5,000 = $15,000 OR 1,000 x $15 = $15,000

Date January 30, 2003	Debit $	Credit $
Retained Earnings	160,000	
Share Capital		100,000
Additional Paid-In Capital		60,000
Explanation: *To record the issue of a 10% common stock dividend on 100,000 outstanding shares at a market price of $16 each.*		

Computation: 100,000 x 10% = $10,000 shares.
10,000 shares x $10 = $100,000
10,000 shares x ($16 - $10) = $60,000
$100,000 + $60,000 = $160,000 OR 10,000 x $16 = $160,000

Date February 28, 2003	Debit $	Credit $
Retained Earnings	220,000	
Dividends Payable		220,000
Explanation: *To record the declaration of a $2 per common share dividend on 110,000* outstanding shares.*		

Computation: 220,000 ÷ 110,000 = $2 per share.

*On January 30, 2003 there were 100,000 common shares outstanding. On that date another 10,000 common shares were issued for a stock dividend. Hence, by February 28, 2003 there are 110,000 common shares outstanding.

Date March 31, 2003	Debit $	Credit $
Income Summary	300,000	
Retained Earnings		300,000
Explanation: To close income summary to retained earnings.		

Date March 31, 2003	Debit $	Credit $
Dividends Payable	220,000	
Cash		220,000
Explanation: To record the payment of a $2 per common share cash dividend on 110,000 outstanding common shares.		

Solution to Question Two

This one is tricky! You must work backwards.

Lowlie Incorporated - General Journal

Date May 25, 2003	Debit $	Credit $
Cash	4,000	
Share Capital		500
Additional Paid-In Capital		3,500
Explanation: To record the issue of 100 common shares at $40 each, par value $5 per share.		

Computation:

Share Capital: $5,500 - $5,000 = $500 worth of $5 par value shares issued. $500 ÷ $5 = 100 shares issued OR 100 shares x $5 = $500.

Additional Paid-In Capital: $33,500 - $30,000 = $3,500 OR 100 shares x ($40 - $5) = $3,500.

Cash: $500 + $3,500 = $4,000

Date December 31, 2003	Debit $	Credit $
Revenues	90,100	
Income Summary		90,100
Explanation: To close revenues to income summary		

Date December 31, 2003	Debit $	Credit $
Income Summary	80,000	
Expenses		80,000
Explanation: *To close expenses to income summary*		

Computation:
Revenues - net income = expenses
$90,100 - $10,100 = $80,000

Date December 31, 2003	Debit $	Credit $
Income Summary	10,100	
Retained Earnings		10,100
Explanation: *To close income summary to retained earnings*		

Date December 31, 2003	Debit $	Credit $
Retained Earnings	2,750	
Dividends Payable		2,750
Explanation: *To record the declaration of a dividend of $2.50 per share on 1,100 outstanding common shares.*		

Computation:
If dividends had not been declared the 2003 retained earnings would increase by net income: that is it should be equal to: $59,100 + $10,100 = $69,200. However, retained earnings is only equal to $66,450. There has been a $69,200 - $66,450 = $2,750 reduction to retained earnings. Thus dividends of $2,750 must have been declared during 2003. Since we have no information regarding when this occurred, we presume it was at the end of the year. Also, the declaration must have been for $2.50 per share. From the share capital account we know there are $5,500 ÷ $5 = 1,100 shares outstanding. The dividend declaration was $2,750. Thus, the per share dividend is calculated: $2,750 ÷ 1,100 = $2.50

Solution to Question Three

Requirement One:

Shellee Corporation - General Journal

Date February 1, 2004	Debit $	Credit $
Retained Earnings	60,000	
Share Capital		60,000
Explanation: To record a 20% stock dividend on 20,000 outstanding common shares at a market value of $15 per share.		

Computation: 20,000 x 20% = 4,000 shares issued.
4,000 x $15 = $60,000

Requirement Two:

Shareholders' Equity before stock dividend	# of shares before stock dividend	Average book value before stock dividend
$115,000 + 103,000 = $218,000	20,000	$218,000 ÷ 20,000 = $10.90

Shareholders' Equity after stock dividend	# of shares after stock dividend	Average book value after stock dividend
$175,000* + 43,000** = $218,000	20,000 + 4,000 = 24,000	$218,000 ÷ 24,000 = $9.08

* $115,000 + $60,000 = $175,000 increase to share capital from the stock dividend.
** $103,000 - $60,000 = $43,000 decrease to retained earnings from the stock dividend.

Requirement Three:

The average book value per share decreased from $10.90 to $9.08. However, there was no dollar effect on either total assets, liabilities or shareholders' equity of Shellee Corporation. The average book value per share declined because there are 4,000 more shares on the same equity value of $218,000. Since the additional stocks have an equal claim on the unchanged equity value, each share must therefore have a lower book value.

Notes
_____
_____
_____
_____
_____
_____
_____
_____
_____
_____
_____
_____
_____
_____
_____
_____
_____
_____
_____
_____
_____
_____
_____
_____
_____
_____
_____
_____
_____
_____
_____
_____
_____

Notes

Notes

_____
_____
_____
_____
_____
_____
_____
_____
_____
_____
_____
_____
_____
_____
_____
_____
_____
_____
_____
_____
_____
_____
_____
_____
_____
_____
_____
_____
_____
_____
_____

Accounting for Corporations

Chapter Five- Statement of Retained Earnings

The Reason for This Chapter

In this chapter we examine a fourth financial statement "the Statement of Retained Earnings".

Why is such a statement necessary? When is it created? What does it tell us? We answer these important questions in Chapter Five along with showing you how we prepare this statement. In addition, we introduce a related topic - Prior Period Adjustments. We close with a new topic - Treasury Shares.

What Do You Already Know?

In this section of the chapter we ask you to complete a pre-test. It will get you thinking about what you already know about accounting. It will also serve as a link between what you learned in Chapters One, Two and Four, and what you are about to learn in Chapter Five. After completing the pre-test, check your answers against the ones provided.

Question One

The Flag Corporation was founded by the Flagler family, over 40 years ago. In recent years the business has grown substantially. At such times it is not uncommon for the company to issue stock dividends in lieu of cash dividends. In the second quarter of 2004, the following transactions affected shareholders' equity. Record these transactions in the general journal of The Flag Corporation. Use the space provided:

Transactions:

April 2, 2004. Declared and issued a 5 percent stock dividend on the common shares. Prior to the stock dividend there were 250,000 shares outstanding with a $3 par value each. On this date each share had a market value of $24.

April 30, 2004. Issued 5,000 common shares for $25 cash per share. The common shares had a par value of $3 per share.

May 11, 2004. Declared a $200,625 cash dividend to all shareholders of record as of June 15, 2004.

June 30, 2004. Closed the income summary balance of $667,000 to retained earnings.

June 30, 2004. Paid the dividend declared on May 11, 2004.

The Flag Corporation - General Journal

Date		Debit $	Credit $
Explanation:			

Computation:

Date	Debit $	Credit $
Explanation:		

Computation:

Date	Debit $	Credit $
Explanation:		

Computation:

Date	Debit $	Credit $
Explanation:		

Date	Debit $	Credit $
Explanation:		

Question Two

If The Flag Corporation's Retained Earnings balance on April 1, 2004 was $2,580,000 what would be the balance on July 1, 2004?

_____

_____

_____

_____

_____

_____

_____

_____

_____

_____

Answer to Question One

The Flag Corporation - General Journal

Date April 2, 2004	Debit $	Credit $
Retained Earnings	300,000	
Share Capital		37,500
Additional Paid-In Capital		262,500
Explanation: To record the issue of a 5% common stock dividend on 250,000 outstanding shares at a market price of $24 per share.		

Computation: 250,000 x 5% = 12,500 shares.
12,500 shares x $3 = $37,500
12,500 shares x ($24 - $3) = $262,500
$37,500 + $262,500 = $300,000 OR 12,500 x $24 = $300,000

Date April 30, 2004	Debit $	Credit $
Cash	125,000	
Share Capital		15,000
Additional Paid-In Capital		110,000
Explanation: To record the issue of 5,000 par value $3 common shares at $25 each.		

Computation: 5,000 x $3 = 15,000
5,000 x ($25 - $3) = $110,000
$15,000 + $110,000 = $125,000 OR 5,000 x $25 = $125,000

Date May 11, 2004	Debit $	Credit $
Retained Earnings	200,625	
Dividends Payable		200,625
Explanation: To record the declaration of a $0.75 per common share dividend on $267,500* outstanding shares.		

Computation: $200,625 ÷ 267,500 = $0.75 per share
*Before April 2, 2004 there were 250,000 common shares outstanding; 12,500 shares were issued on that date for the stock dividend. On April 30, 2004 another 5,000 shares were issued. Hence, by May 11, 2004 there are 267,500 shares outstanding.

Date June 30, 2004	Debit $	Credit $
Income Summary	667,000	
Retained Earnings		667,000
Explanation: To close income summary to retained earnings		

Date June 30, 2004	Debit $	Credit $
Dividends Payable	200,625	
Cash		200,625
Explanation: To record the payment of a $0.75 per common share cash dividend on 267,500 outstanding shares.		

Answer to Question Two

On July 1, 2004 the balance in Retained Earnings would be $2,746,375.
The change was a result of:

Stock Dividend	-$300,000
Cash Dividend	-$200,625
Income Summary	$667,000
TOTAL change	$166,375

Thus, $2,580,000 + $166,375 = $2,746,375

Notice, the multiple entries make it more difficult to understand why the retained earnings balance changed. Preparing a Statement of Retained Earnings provides detailed information. This statement helps the users of financial statements understand what happened to the Retained Earnings account during the accounting period. This is the main topic of this chapter.

How This Chapter Relates to Other Chapters in This Book

In Chapter One we accounted for selling shares by using the Share Capital account. In this chapter we account for the corporation buying back its shares. We call these Treasury Shares.

Throughout this book we have examined a variety of transactions affecting Shareholders' Equity. Chapter Two transferred net income onto the balance sheet through the Retained Earnings account. In Chapter Four we reduced Retained Earnings to account for dividend declarations. These numerous equity transactions may occur during any accounting period. Multiple transactions make it difficult for investors to understand why Retained Earnings changed during the period unless the transactions are summarized and presented in a meaningful way. In order to clarify why Retained Earnings changes during the accounting period, this chapter presents the Statement of Retained Earnings.

What Are the Topics in This Chapter?

As you know, from the perspective of balance sheet presentation, the main difference between Corporations and the other forms of business can be found in the Equity Section of the balance sheet. In keeping with this theme, we introduce Treasury Shares and present a new financial statement - the Statement of Retained Earnings. In addition, we examine a related topic, prior period adjustments.

Topics Covered in Chapter Five   Level of Importance

Why Prepare a Statement of Retained Earnings?	
Understanding Information	***
What Does a Statement of Retained Earnings Report?	
Net Income	***
Dividends	***
Errors and Changes in Accounting Policy	*
Preparing the Statement of Retained Earnings	
Matching the dates	***
The Link to other Financial Statements	***
The Statement of Retained Earnings	***
Prior Period Adjustments	
Errors	**
Changes in Accounting Policy	**
Treasury Shares	
Definition	***
Why Repurchase Shares?	**
Authorized Shares	**
Accounting for Cancelled Treasury Shares	***
Accounting for Treasury Shares	*
Account Structures for Different Business Types	
A Summary	***

Why Prepare a Statement of Retained Earnings?

Understanding Information

Accounting must provide information that is useful. In addition to meeting regulatory requirements, this may help attract new investors and retain existing ones. Useful information provides insight into how well a firm has done, is doing and can be expected to do. Therefore, investors use accounting information to make decisions about the past, present and future performance of the business.

The financial statements provide this information. Each financial statement contains specific information. The Income Statement informs us as to the profitability during a period, the Balance sheet tells us about the investments and claims at a particular date, and the Statement of Cash Flows details what happened to cash during a period. We will use the Statement of Retained Earnings to communicate the causes for changes to the Retained Earnings account for a particular period. This financial statement provides a complete description of how the account changed.

Unlike the other three statements, the Statement of Retained Earnings is not required. However, most corporations include it because investors want to understand what caused the Retained Earnings account to change. To do so is useful.

What Does a Statement of Retained Earnings Report?

The Retained Earnings account is one of the two basic components of equity. The Statement of Retained Earnings reveals the specific changes to this account during an accounting period. During any period it can increase, or decrease for a variety of reasons. Usually, the change is a combined result of Net Income or Loss, Dividend declarations and errors or changes in certain accounting policies. We will discuss each in turn.

Net Income

During each accounting period the income statement reports either a profit or loss (unless, of course, the company "broke even"). We transfer the income statement result to Retained Earnings via the Income Summary account. Profits increase Retained Earnings while losses reduce it. The Statement of Retained Earnings reports the net income or loss as one of the changes to Retained Earnings during the accounting period.

Dividends

Traditionally, the corporation declares a dividend payment every three months. Dividends are a reward for ownership. They can be paid either with cash or shares. In both cases, dividends require a reduction to Retained Earnings. The Statement of Retained Earnings reports the dividend declarations as one of the changes to Retained Earnings during the accounting period

Errors and Changes in Accounting Policy

Sometimes a future decision changes what was reported in the past. Discovery of accounting errors or changes to certain accounting policies both result in the need to adjust previously reported amounts. We refer to these changes as Prior Period Adjustments. We examine this topic in detail later in this chapter.

At this point we simply note that changes to financial statements issued in the past are reflected in the financial statements for the current period. We indicate prior period adjustments by changing the Retained Earnings account in the current period. Thus, the Statement of Retained Earnings must report any prior period adjustments during the accounting period.

Preparing a Statement of Retained Earnings

Matching the Dates

We prepare the Statement of Retained Earnings on the same date as the other financial statements. Doing so captures the complete performance of the business for a specific accounting period. Since we use this statement to communicate the changes to Retained Earnings, its date must match the period during which the Retained Earnings account changed. Public corporations prepare the financial statements every quarter. All corporations prepare their financial statements at least annually.

The Link to Other Financial Statements

The statement of retained earnings provides a complete description of changes to Retained Earnings during the accounting period. Every change is captured in part on each financial statement. The link between the Statement of Retained Earnings and the other financial statements is as follows:

When constructing the Statement of Retained Earnings we begin with the Retained Earnings balance at the beginning of the accounting period. To it, we add the net income from the income statement. Of course, we would deduct a net loss. Next we subtract the dividend declaration. We note any cash dividend payments on the Statement of Cash Flows as Cash used in Financing. The final Retained Earnings balance on both the Balance Sheet and Statement of Retained Earnings is the same.

The following diagram shows the link between all four financial statements:

Link between all four financial statements

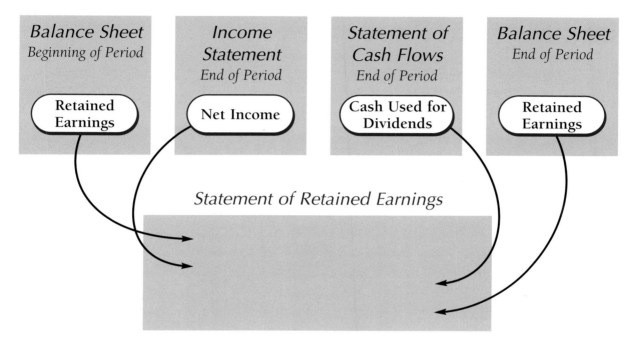

The Statement of Retained Earnings

The following table depicts a typical Statement of Retained Earnings. We obtained the information from The Flag Corporation's second quarter, contained in the Self-Test at the beginning of this chapter:

The Flag Corporation
Statement of Retained Earnings
For the three months ending June 30, 2004

Retained Earnings balance, April 1, 2004	$2,580,000
Net Income for the second quarter	667,000
Subtotal	3,247,000
Deduct dividends declared during the quarter:	
Stock Dividend $300,000	
Cash Dividend 200,625	500,625
Retained Earnings balance, June 30, 2004	**$2,746,375**

Test your understanding of the link between the financial statements while you practice preparing a Statement of Retained Earnings. Try Exercise One.

Now You Try It

Exercise One

The bookkeeper for Carpets Inc. has provided the following account balances:

Account	Balance	Date
Retained Earnings	$214,485	December 31, 2003
Revenues	54,268	December 31, 2004
Accounts Receivable	21,485	December 31, 2004
Retained Earnings	224,967	December 31, 2004
Expenses	38,786	December 31, 2004
Bank Loan	66,450	December 31, 2004
Cash	2,450	December 31, 2004

Select the appropriate accounts and their values. Use the space provided below to prepare the Statement of Retained Earnings for Carpets Inc.. Hint: you will have to compute some of the values you need!

Carpets Inc.
Statement of Retained Earnings
For the _____

Subtotal		

Computation:

Answers

Answer to Exercise One

Carpets Inc.
Statement of Retained Earnings
For the year ending December 31, 2004

Retained Earnings balance, December 31, 2003	$214,485
Net Income for the year*	15,482
Subtotal	229,967
Deduct dividends declared during the the year**	5,000
Retained Earnings balance, December 31, 2004	**$224,967**

Computation:

* $54,268 - $38,786 = $15,482 net income.

** $229,967 - $224,967 = $5,000 dividends declared.

Prior Period Adjustments

These adjustments recognize the effects of making a change to a past financial statement. We reflect the change by making an adjustment to the Retained Earnings account. Prior Period Adjustments are the result of correcting errors or changes in certain accounting policies. We examine each, next.

Errors

The accounting system contains many safeguards to protect against errors. We use a double entry debit/credit system along with periodic trial balances to ensure that journal entries and ledger postings are error-free. While errors are uncommon in a good accounting system, they may still happen.

Any accounting errors discovered during the accounting period are corrected in that period. Errors discovered once the period has passed must still be corrected.

We cannot simply amend the accounts of a prior year because the books for all prior years have already been closed. We correct errors from prior years by making an adjustment to the opening balance of Retained Earnings. We change or restate the beginning value of Retained Earnings in the current accounting period by the amount of the error.

Why adjust Retained Earnings? The result of any transaction ultimately affects shareholders' equity. We reserve the Share Capital account for recording share issuance. Retained Earnings captures the operating results. Revenues increase Retained Earnings, while expenses reduce Retained Earnings. Thus, it is easiest to reflect the impact of a previous error by calculating its effect on shareholders' equity and adjusting the Retained Earnings account.

Why restate the beginning balance? The error took place in a past accounting period. Adjusting this period's results would be inappropriate. The error should not impact this period's net income as it was not a result of this period's operations. By restating Retained Earnings at the beginning of this period we clearly show the change is a result of a prior period.

The impact of an income-related error is that either an improper gain or loss was recorded in the year of the error. Once the amount of the error is determined we record the correction in a special account and close it directly to Retained Earnings in the year that the error is discovered. Errors which originally caused gains to be improperly recorded would decrease Retained Earnings when they are corrected. Errors which caused losses to be improperly recorded would increase Retained Earnings when they are corrected. Since we close the result directly to Retained Earnings it must be net of income taxes. The adjustment is captured on the Statement of Retained Earnings.

Preparing the journal entries for prior period adjustment requires some sophistication. Instead of practicing these entries, we only ask you to be familiar with the effect on the Statement of Retained Earnings.

Try Exercise Two to practice reporting errors from prior periods.

Now You Try It

Exercise Two

Lifter's Limited has just reported net income of $21,589 for the year ending December 31, 2004. During the year the company declared and paid dividends amounting to $5,300. The balance in the Retained Earnings account as at December 31, 2003 is $250,400. During the current year the accountant for Lifter's Limited discovered an error from the previous year. No adjustments have yet been made. The error resulted in the recording of an incorrect gain of $4,800, on an after-tax basis, in the prior year.

Use the space provided below to assist you in preparing a statement of retained earnings for Lifter's Limited. Remember you must restate the beginning Retained Earnings balance to account for the error.

Carpets Inc.
Statement of Retained Earnings
For the _____

Retained Earnings balance, December 31, 2003	$
Prior Period Adjustment:	
Balance as restated	
Net Income for the year	
Subtotal	
Deduct dividends declared during the year	
Retained Earnings balance, December 31, 2004	

Answers

Answer to Exercise Two

Carpets Inc.
Statement of Retained Earnings
For the year ending December 31, 2004

Retained Earnings balance, December 31, 2003	$250,400
Prior Period Adjustment:	
Less: adjustment for correction of prior year's accounting error, net of tax.	4,800
Balance as restated	245,600
Net Income for the year	21,589
Subtotal	267,189
Deduct dividends declared during the the year	5,300
Retained Earnings balance, December 31, 2004	**$261,889**

A deduction is made because the error caused an improper gain to be recorded in the prior year. Note that an improper loss recorded in a prior year would require an addition to the opening balance of retained earnings.

Changes in Accounting Policy

Changes in accounting policy generally fall into two categories: 1) those that result from adopting new accounting standards required by the profession and 2) those that result from changing one generally accepted standard to another accepted standard. Discussion of how we account for changes in accounting policy is far beyond the scope of this book.

In some countries, changing from an incorrect accounting policy to a correct accounting policy is not considered to be a change in accounting policy. Rather, such a change is accounted for as the correction of an accounting error.

Treasury Shares

Definition

Most jurisdictions will allow corporations to purchase their own outstanding shares. While some legal restrictions do apply, Treasury stocks are shares that have been issued, sold and re-purchased by the corporation. When a company buys back its own stocks, we think of these shares as being held in the company's treasury. They are simply shares waiting to be re-used. Sometimes they are cancelled.

Treasury shares are no longer outstanding. This means they do not receive dividends, have voting rights or enjoy any other shareholder rights. They are shares that are issued, but they are not in the hands of shareholders.

Why Repurchase Shares?

Many sound business reasons exist as to why a corporation may repurchase its own shares. While the reasons are complicated, we attempt to simplify them without detailed explanation, as follows:

1. It may be desirable to change the ownership structure.
2. Shares may be needed to satisfy employee bonus plans.
3. Shares may be needed to acquire another company.
4. Shares may be needed to settle a claim against the company.

By reducing the number of outstanding shares, the percentage of shares held by each shareholder will change. Should this prove to be desirable, the corporation may achieve it by repurchasing it own shares and holding them as Treasury Shares. This satisfies the first reason.

What about reasons two, three and four? If the corporation needs more shares, must they repurchase them? This depends on the status of its authorized shares. We examine it next.

Authorized Shares

Recall that the certificate of incorporation clearly states the maximum number of shares that may be issued. This number is not easily changed. Should the corporation anticipate the need for more shares, they may have to repurchase them. Once repurchased, these Treasury shares can be put to other uses in the future; they can be given to employees, given to other companies or used to settle a legal claim.

Sometimes the certificate of incorporation authorizes an unlimited number of shares. In this instance there is really no need for Treasury Shares. While the company may still repurchase its shares, instead of being held in the Treasury they will simply be cancelled.

Accounting for Cancelled Treasury Shares

When authorized shares are unlimited, the journal entries for Treasury shares are simply the reverse of those for share issuance, if the same amount of cash is involved. The company uses its cash to pay shareholders for the repurchase of their shares. Because these shares are being cancelled, the number of shares and value of share capital will be reduced accordingly. Of course, when the share capital has a par value, the additional paid-in capital account must also be reduced for the excess over par paid for the repurchase.

Try Exercises Three and Four to practice the journal entries for a share repurchase when authorized shares are unlimited.

Now You Try It

Exercise Three

The certificate of incorporation for Recycling Incorporated states it has an unlimited number of no-par authorized common shares. As a result of several stock dividend issues, the company now finds they have a number of stockholders holding a small amount of shares. The company finds this undesirable, as these shareholders are expensive to maintain.

Recycling Incorporated approached these shareholders with an offer to buy back their shares at a price of $22 each. The offer was accepted. Specifically, there were 150 shareholders holding 5 shares each. Today is June 15, 2004. Use the space provided to record the treasury share repurchase and cancellation. Assume that the shares were originally issued for $22 per share.

Recycling Incorporated - General Journal

Date	Debit $	Credit $
Explanation:		

Computation:

Answers

Answer to Exercise Three

Recycling Incorporated - General Journal

Date June 15, 2004	Debit $	Credit $
Share Capital	16,500	
Cash		16,500
Explanation: To record the repurchase and cancellation of 750 common shares at $22 each.		

Computation: 150 x 5 = 750 shares repurchased.
750 x $22 = $16,500 cost.

Now You Try It

Exercise Four

The certificate of incorporation for Recovery Incorporated states it has an unlimited number of $2 par-value authorized common shares. As a result of several stock dividend issues, the company now finds they have a number of stockholders holding a small amount of shares. The company finds this undesirable, as these shareholders are expensive to maintain.

Recovery Incorporated approached these shareholders with an offer to buy back their shares at a price of $25 each. The offer was accepted. Specifically, there were 100 shareholders holding 3 shares each. Today is September 15, 2004. Use the space provided to record the treasury share repurchase and cancellation. Assume that the shares were originally issued for $25 per share.

Recovery Incorporated - General Journal

Date		Debit $	Credit $
Explanation:			

Computation:

Answers

Answer to Exercise Four

Recovery Incorporated - General Journal

Date September 15, 2004	Debit $	Credit $
Share Capital	$600	
Additional Paid-In Capital	6,900	
Cash		$7,500
Explanation: *To record the repurchase and cancellation of 300 $2 par-value common shares at $25 each.*		

Computation: *100 x 3 = 300 shares repurchased.*
   300 x $2 = $600
   300 x ($25 - $2) = $6,900 additional Paid-In Capital
            $7,500 cash OR 300 x $25 = $7,500

What would happen if the amount of additional paid-in capital was not sufficient to cover the cost of the share repurchase? While this situation is rare and would be subject to several legal restrictions, it is still possible.

When the value of Additional Paid-In Capital is insufficient for the share repurchase, we remove the excess from Retained Earnings.

Consider the following example:

The certificate of incorporation for Retroactive Incorporated states it has an unlimited number of $10 par-value authorized common shares. The performance of the company was very stable until recently. Excess earnings have caused the stock price to soar.

Retroactive Incorporated made an offer to repurchase 1,000 of its shares but will have to pay a price of $50 each. The balance in the Additional Paid-In Capital account was $30,000 immediately before this offer was accepted by the shareholders. The transaction is as follows:

1,000 x $50 = $50,000 cash worth of shares repurchased
1,000 x $10 = $10,000 share capital
1,000 x ($50 - $10) = $40,000 additional paid-in capital

A problem arises because there is insufficient Additional Paid-In Capital to account for this transaction. With only $30,000 available in this account, it is short by $10,000. We resolve the problem by taking the excess needed from another shareholders' equity account; Retained Earnings. The transaction would be recorded as follows:

Retroactive Incorporated - General Journal

Date date of Treasury Stock transaction	Debit $	Credit $
Share Capital	10,000	
Additional Paid-In Capital	30,000	
Retained Earnings	10,000	
Cash		50,000
Explanation: to record a treasury share repurchase and cancellation of 1,000 $10 par-value common shares at $50 each.		

Since this transaction affected Retained Earnings, we report it in the statement of retained earnings. The reduction would be explained as the result of a Treasury Stock transaction. Note that the reduction in cash is the same as the reduction in total shareholders' equity, but in this case three shareholders' equity accounts were affected, not two.

As you can see, Treasury Share transactions can become complex. In fact, we have really only introduced this advanced topic. It becomes even more intricate when the number of authorized shares is limited.

Accounting for Treasury Shares

When the number of authorized shares is limited, accounting for a share repurchase becomes very complicated. Since these shares will be available for re-issue, we must keep track of them. A contra account called Treasury Shares will be created. This account will be reported on the balance sheet as a reduction within the shareholders' equity section.

Due to the complex nature of accounting for Treasury Shares when authorized shares are limited, we end our discussion here. Nevertheless, the information covered thus far is enough to ensure a basic appreciation of this advanced topic.

Account Structures for Different Business Types

A Summary

Although there are three forms of business organizations, the fundamentals of accounting and reporting for each are the same, except with respect to equity. As a review, we have summarized their similarities and differences. The following table compares the typical account structure for each business type:

Typical Account Structure

Corporation (Shareholders' Equity)	Sole Proprietorship (Owners' Equity)	Partnership (Partners' Equity)
Share Capital Additional Paid-In Capital	Owner's name, Capital	Partner A, Capital Partner B, Capital
Retained Earnings	Not used	Not used
Dividends	Owner's name, Withdrawals	Partner A, Withdrawals Partner B, Withdrawals
Income Summary (closed to Retained Earnings)	Income Summary (closed to Owner's name, Capital)	Income Summary (closed to Partner A, Capital and Partner B, Capital)
Treasury Shares	Not used	Not used
Revenues, Expenses, Gains and Losses	Same	Same
Assets and Liabilities	Same	Same

Can you match a journal entry to its business type? Try Exercise Five.

Now You Try It

Exercise Five

For each of the following journal entries, state whether it applies to a corporation, sole proprietorship, partnership or a combination of business types. Provide a brief explanation.

Entry One	Debit $	Credit $
Income Summary	667,000	
Retained Earnings		667,000

TYPE: _____

Entry Two	Debit $	Credit $
Cash	5,000	
Peter Able, Withdrawals		5,000

TYPE: _____

Entry Three	Debit $	Credit $
Income Summary	52,000	
Jane Doer, Capital		26,000
James Donner, Capital		26,000

TYPE: _____

Entry Four	Debit $	Credit $
Retained Earnings	20,000	
Dividends Payable		20,000

TYPE: _____

Entry Five	Debit $	Credit $
Income Summary	32,000	
Francis Drake, Capital		32,000

TYPE: _____

Answers

Answer to Exercise Five

Entry One: Corporation. Only corporations use Retained Earnings.

Entry Two: Partnership or Sole Proprietorship. They both use Withdrawals. It is possible that only one partner is making a withdrawal.

Entry Three: Partnership. Income Summary is closed to more than one capital account.

Entry Four: Corporation. Only corporations make dividend declarations and payments.

Entry Five: Sole Proprietorship. Income Summary is closed to one capital account only. If it were a partnership more than one capital account would be used.

What You Have Learned in This Chapter

This chapter represents an accounting summary of corporate equity. We presented a fourth financial statement - the statement of retained earnings. We demonstrated how to prepare this statement. We also examined how this statement helps shareholders to understand the changes to retained earnings during an accounting period.

A related topic, prior period adjustments, enables us to appreciate how accountants report the correction of errors which occurred in earlier accounting periods. They must adjust the Retained Earnings account at the beginning of the current period. Doing so corrects the error without affecting the current year's operating results.

Finally, Chapter Twenty-three presented a new topic - Treasury Shares. While the nature of this subject is somewhat difficult, the overview presented gives the reader a basic understanding of the topic.

Important Terms in This Chapter

Cancelled Treasury Shares: when authorized shares are unlimited, the repurchased or Treasury Shares are simply cancelled.

Net of income taxes: after-tax. An amount that has been adjusted for income taxes.

Prior Period Adjustments: adjustments made in the current period as a result of accounting errors which occurred in a prior year or, in rare cases, changes in accounting policy during the current period. The adjustment results in a change to the opening balance of retained earnings in the current period if it is income-related.

Restating: changing retroactively. We apply changes to specific accounts or financial statements as a result of correcting errors in previously issued financial statements, or in rare cases, as a result of changes in accounting policy.

Standards: accounting rules or principles used in transaction analysis.

Statement of Retained Earnings: a financial statement that is not required, but is useful because it reports the causes of changes to Retained Earnings.

Treasury Shares: shares of a corporation repurchased by the issuing corporation. Until such shares are cancelled they are considered to be issued but not outstanding, since they are not actually in the hands of shareholders.

Should You Move on to the Next Chapter?

Now it's time to check and see how comfortable you are with your new knowledge. Perform the Self-Test to verify whether you should move on, or go back and review the information contained in this chapter.

Self-Test for Chapter Five

Question One

In the space provided, name the appropriate business type for each account name. For accounts used by all business types write "ALL". We have completed the first one for you:

Account Name	Business Type
Share Capital	*Corporation*
Dividends Payable	
Wage Expense	
Treasury Shares	
Income Summary	
Prepaid Insurance	
Retained Earnings	
Withdrawals	
Accounts Receivable	

Question Two

What is a prior period adjustment? How do we account for it?

_____
_____
_____
_____
_____
_____
_____
_____
_____
_____
_____
_____
_____
_____

Question Three

What are Treasury Shares? How do we account for them?

_____
_____
_____
_____
_____
_____
_____
_____
_____
_____
_____
_____
_____
_____

Question Four

The following account balances were selected from the records of Biglow Corporation at December 31, 2004, after all adjusting entries were completed:

Account	Amount
Share Capital Common Stock, no par, unlimited number authorized, 119,500 shares outstanding	$780,000
Dividends declared and paid during 2004	34,000
Retained Earnings, January 1, 2004	80,000
Income Summary for 2004 (credit balance)	35,000
Correction of prior year's accounting error (a debit in the current year)	10,000

Based on the above information prepare a statement of retained earnings for 2004 and the shareholders' equity section of the balance sheet at December 31, 2004. Use the space provided below:

Biglow Corporation
Statement of Retained Earnings
For the _____

Balance as restated	
Subtotal	

Computations:

Biglow Corporation
Balance Sheet - Shareholders' Equity section
As at _____

Shareholders' Equity	
Total Shareholders' Equity	

Computations:

Answers to Self-Test for Chapter Five

Answer to Question One

Account Name	Business Type
Share Capital	Corporation
Dividends Payable	Corporation
Wage Expense	ALL
Treasury Shares	Corporation
Income Summary	ALL
Prepaid Insurance	ALL
Retained Earnings	Corporation
Withdrawals	Sole Proprietorship, Partnership
Accounts Receivable	ALL

Answer to Question Two

Sometimes a future decision changes what was reported in the past. Discovery of accounting errors or changes to certain accounting policies both result in the need to adjust previously reported amounts. We refer to these changes as Prior Period Adjustments. We restate the beginning value of Retained Earnings during the current accounting period for the amount of the prior period adjustment(s).

The impact of an income-related error is that either an improper gain or loss was recorded in the year of the error. Once the amount of the error is determined we record the correction in a special account and close it directly to Retained Earnings in the year that the error is discovered. Errors which originally caused gains to be improperly recorded would decrease Retained Earnings when they are corrected. Errors which caused losses to be improperly recorded would increase Retained Earnings when they are corrected. Since we close the result directly to Retained Earnings it must be net of income taxes. The adjustment is captured on the Statement of Retained Earnings.

Answer to Question Three

Treasury shares are shares that have been issued, sold and re-purchased by the corporation but have not yet been cancelled. When a company buys back its own stocks, we think of these shares as being held in the company's treasury. They are simply shares waiting to be re-issued or cancelled.

Treasury shares are no longer outstanding. This means no dividends, voting rights or other shareholder rights apply to such shares. They are shares that are issued, but they are not in the hands of shareholders. Therefore they are no longer outstanding.

When the certificate of incorporation states that the number of authorized shares is unlimited, we generally cancel the re-acquired shares. The journal entries are opposite those for issuance of the shares assuming that the shares are repurchased for the same amount for which they were originally issued. When the number of authorized shares is limited, the accounting entries become more complicated. The Treasury shares will often not be cancelled. They will be held in a special Treasury Shares account and reported on the balance sheet as a deduction from shareholders' equity.

Answer to Question Four

Biglow Corporation
Statement of Retained Earnings
For the year ended December 31, 2004

Retained Earnings balance, January 1, 2004	$80,000
Prior Period Adjustment: *Deduct adjustment for correction of prior year's accounting error, net of tax.	*10,000
Balance as restated	70,000
Net Income for the year	35,000
Subtotal	105,000
Deduct dividends declared during the the year	34,000
Retained Earnings balance, December 31, 2004	**$71,000**

Computations:
* must be deducted since it is a debit. We are reversing the gain improperly recorded in an earlier year.

Biglow Corporation
Balance Sheet - Shareholders' Equity section
As at December 31, 2004

Shareholders' Equity	
Share Capital, no par, unlimited number authorized, 119,500 shares outstanding	$780,000
*Retained Earnings	71,000
Total Shareholders' Equity	**$851,000**

Computations:
* from statement of retained earnings.

Practice Problems for Chapter Five

Question One

Detailed Incorporated has completed all of the annual information processing at December 31, 2004, except for the preparation of the financial statements. The following relevant account balances were reflected at that date:

Detailed Incorporated
Excerpts from the Adjusted Trial Balance
As at December 31, 2004

Account	Debit $	Credit $
Cash	56,000	
Accounts Receivable	42,000	
Supplies Inventory	40,000	
Equipment	196,000	
Accumulated Depreciation - Equipment		10,000
Accounts Payable		42,000
Income Taxes Payable		9,000
Bank Loan		65,000
Share Capital, no par, unlimited number authorized, 125,000 shares outstanding		100,000
Retained Earnings (January 1, 2004)		152,000

In addition, the following information pertaining to activities during 2004 is as follows:

• Net Income was $66,000.

• Cash Dividends declared and paid during the year amounted to $12,000.

• Common Stock Dividends declared and distributed during the year amounted to $88,000 (relates to 11,000 additional common shares distributed).

• An accounting error made in 2003 was discovered. The error caused a $10,000 gain, after tax, to be improperly recorded in 2003.

Required:

Prepare a statement of retained earnings for the year ended December 31, 2004, and a classified balance sheet as at December 31, 2004. Use the space provided below:

Detailed Incorporated
Statement of Retained Earnings
For the _____

Subtotal		
Retained Earnings balance, December 31, 2004		

Computations:

Detailed Incorporated
Balance Sheet
As at _____

Assets	Liabilities
	TOTAL (Liabilities)
	Shareholders' Equity
	TOTAL (Shareholders' Equity)
TOTAL (Assets)	**TOTAL** (Liabilities and Shareholders' Equity)

Computation:

Notes

_____
_____
_____
_____
_____
_____
_____
_____
_____
_____
_____
_____
_____

Question Two

The bookkeeper for Bungled Corporation prepared the following
<u>incorrect</u> balance sheet:

Bungled Corporation
Balance Sheet
For the Year ending December 31, 2004

Assets		Liabilities	
Cash	$27,000	Due in one year	12,000
Account Receivable	25,000	Due later	56,000
Supplies Inventory	61,000	**Capital**	
Equipment (net of depreciation reserves $75,000)	210,000	Stocks, 60,000, par-value $2	120,000
		Stocks, premium	30,000
		Net income from 2003	7,000
		Net income from previous years (not including 2003)	70,000
		Correction of error which occured a year ago (a credit, net of tax, in the current year)	2,000
		Cash dividends paid during the year	14,000
		Profits for the year 2004	40,000
TOTAL (Debits)	323,000	**TOTAL** (Credits)	351,000

Required:

1. List all the errors or deficiencies you can identify in the balance
   sheet. Assume the values given are correct.

2. Prepare a <u>correct</u> statement of retained earnings for 2004.

3. Prepare a <u>correct</u> balance sheet in good form.

You may use the space provided below:

Requirement One: (we found sixteen errors!)

1. _____
2. _____
3. _____
4. _____
5. _____
6. _____
7. _____
8. _____
9. _____
10. _____
11. _____
12. _____
13. _____
14. _____
15. _____
16. _____

Requirement Two:

Bungled Corporation
Statement of Retained Earnings

Balance as restated	
Subtotal	

Computations:

Requirement Three:

Bungled Corporation
Balance Sheet

Assets	Liabilities

Solutions to Practice Problems for Chapter Five

Solution to Question One

Detailed Incorporated
Statement of Retained Earnings
For the year ended December 31, 2004

Retained Earnings balance, January 1, 2004	$152,000
Prior Period Adjustment:	
*Deduct adjustment for correction of prior year's accounting error, net of tax.	10,000*
Balance as restated	142,000
Net Income for the year	66,000
Subtotal	208,000
Deduct dividends declared during the the year:	
Cash Dividends $12,000	
Common Stock Dividends $88,000	100,000
Retained Earnings balance, December 31, 2004	**$108,000**

Computations:
* must be deducted since it is a debit. We had improperly recorded it as a gain in the previous year.

Detailed Incorporated
Balance Sheet
As at December 31, 2004

Assets		Liabilities	
Cash	$56,000	Accounts Payable	42,000
Account Receivable	42,000	Income Taxes Payable	9,000
Supplies Inventory	40,000	Bank Loan	65,000
Equipment	196,000	**TOTAL** (Liabilities)	**116,000**
Less: Accumulated Depreciation	(10,000)		
		Shareholders' Equity	
		*Share Capital, no-par,	
		unlimited number authorized,	
		125,000 shares outstanding	100,000
		**Retained Earnings	108,000
		TOTAL (Shareholders' Equity)	**208,000**
TOTAL (Assets)	**324,000**	**TOTAL** (Liabilities and Shareholders' Equity)	**324,000**

Computation:

*No adjustment needed, as there were 125,000 shares outstanding on December 31, 2004. The stock dividend took place during the year and is included in this amount.
**from the statement of retained earnings.

Answer to Question Two

Requirement One:

Errors made in the balance sheet preparation are as follows:

1. The heading is incorrect: it should read "as at December 31, 2004".
2. Information belonging on the statement of retained earnings has been included in the balance sheet: dividends, net income and the prior period adjustment should not be shown on the balance sheet.
3. Accumulated Depreciation has not been shown separately.
4. The proper term for depreciation on the balance sheet is "accumulated depreciation".

5. The word debit has been used instead of assets
6. The word credit has been used instead of Shareholders Equity and Liabilities.
7. The liabilities have been named according to their due dates. The words Current and Long-term are preferable.
8. The Liabilities have not been totalled.
9. The word Capital is used in place of Shareholders' Equity.
10. The word stock is used in place of the Share Capital account.
11. The words stock premium is used in place of Additional Paid-In Capital.
12. Net income from previous years should be called Retained Earnings.
13. Net income from 2003 should be included in Retained Earnings.
14. The word Profits should be replaced by Net Income, and should not be shown on the balance sheet.
15. Dividends have been *added* to shareholders' equity, and should not be shown on the balance sheet.
16. The balance sheet does not balance!

Requirement Two

Bungled Corporation
Statement of Retained Earnings
For the year ending December 31, 2004

Retained Earnings balance, January 1, 2004	$77,000*
Prior Period Adjustment:	
Add adjustment for correction of prior year's accounting error, net of tax.	2,000**
Balance as restated	79,000
Net Income for the year	40,000
Subtotal	119,000
Deduct dividends declared during the the year	14,000
Retained Earnings balance, December 31, 2004	**$105,000**

Computations:
* $70,000 + $7,000 = $77,000
** *must be added since it is a credit. We must reverse the debit or loss improperly recorded in the prior year.*

Requirement Three
Corrections shown in bold italics:

Bungled Corporation
Balance Sheet
As at December 31, 2004

Assets		Liabilities	
Cash	$27,000	**Current liabilities**	12,000
Account Receivable	25,000	**Long-term liabilities**	56,000
Supplies Inventory	61,000	**TOTAL** (Liabilities)	**68,000**
Equipment	**285,000***		
Less: accumulated depreciation	**(75,000)**	**Shareholders' Equity**	
		Share Capital, 60,000 $2 par-value common shares outstanding	120,000
		Additional Paid-In Capital	30,000
		Retained Earnings	105,000
		TOTAL (Shareholders' Equity)	255,000
TOTAL (Assets)	323,000	**TOTAL** (Liabilities and Shareholders' Equity)	323,000

* $210,000 + $75,000 = $285,000. *Since the equipment was incorrectly shown on the balance sheet net of accumulated depreciation, we must add it back to show the full acquisition cost.*

Notes

_____

_____

_____

_____

_____

_____

_____

_____

_____

_____

Notes

Accounting for Corporations

Chapter Six - Preparing Financial Statements for a Corporation

The Reason for This Chapter

Can you prepare all four financial statements for a corporation? This chapter gives you the opportunity to practice preparing these important financial statements. You must rely on the accounting knowledge gained in Fundamentals of Accounting: Volumes One, Two, Three; and Accounting for Corporations: Volume One.

This Chapter consists of two separate case studies, each involving a different company. Each company operates a business, but they need help with their books. As an accountant, you will provide this aid.

In each case we will provide you with transactions, dates, and a brief summary of the company. To guide you through the accounting process we have provided blank forms for each case. All you must do is complete the forms provided!

What Do You Already Know?

In this section of the chapter we ask you to complete a pre-test. We will test your ability to prepare a Statement of Cash Flows.

This statement was introduced in Volume Three. While we have referred to it in this book, we have not reviewed it. For your convenience, we have added a brief summary of this statement, as follows:

The Statement of Cash Flows examines how cash changes during an accounting period. This makes it similar to the Income Statement. However, because the Statement of Cash Flows focuses on cash and not revenues or expenses, it is different from the Income Statement. Remember, the Income Statement captures revenues when they are earned and expenses when they are incurred. This probably differs from the time that cash is actually exchanged.

We calculate how the cash changes in a company by using the following equation:

CASH SOURCES - CASH USES = CHANGE IN CASH

Cash sources show where the money comes from. We may also refer to them as cash inflows or increases. Cash uses show where the money goes. We may also call them cash outflows or decreases. The difference between the two is the change in cash.

We divide the Statement of Cash Flows into five sections:

1. Operating Cash Flows
2. Investing Cash Flows
3. Financing Cash Flows
4. Change in Cash
5. Proving the Cash Balance

Prepare a statement of cash flows. Complete the pre-test. If you have difficulties with it, you should go back and review this topic. After completing the pre-test, check your answers against the ones provided. If they are correct, then complete the cases in this chapter.

Question One

The year 2003 income statement for the Castings Corporation showed sales revenues of $600,000 and expenses - including depreciation, of $400,000. This resulted in net income of $200,000 for that year. Assume all corporate sales are on a cash-only basis and all operating expenses are paid with cash. The following additional facts from year 2003 are also available:

Dividends declared and paid	$10,000
Depreciation expense	40,000
Purchase of machinery for cash	320,000
10,000 no-par shares issued and sold for $10 each	100,000
Obtained a bank loan	50,000
Cash on Balance Sheet, December 31, 2003	85,000
Cash on Balance Sheet, January 1, 2003	25,000

How did the Castings Corporation receive and use cash during year 2003? To answer, prepare a Statement of Cash Flows. Demonstrate that the ending cash balance equals the amount shown on the Balance Sheet. Use the space provided below:

Castings Corporation
Statement of Cash Flows
For the year ended December 31, 2003

	Sub-totals	Totals
Cash from Operations		
Change in cash from operating activities:		
Cash from Investing		
Change in cash from investing activities		
Cash from Financing		
Change in cash from financing activities		
Total change in cash during the year		
Proof:		
Beginning cash balance (January 1, 2003)		
Total change in cash during the year		
Ending cash balance (December 31, 2003)		

Answer to Question One

Castings Corporation
Statement of Cash Flows
For the year ended December 31, 2003

	Sub-totals	Totals
Cash from Operations		
Cash from revenues	$600,000	
Cash used for expenses*	(360,000)	
Change in cash from operating activities:		$240,000
Cash from Investing		
Purchase of machinery	(320,000)	
Change in cash from investing activities		(320,000)
Cash from Financing		
Dividends declared and paid	(10,000)	
Issuance of 10,000 shares at $10 each	100,000	
Bank Loan	50,000	
Change in cash from financing activities		140,000
Total change in cash during the year		**$ 60,000**
Proof:		
Beginning cash balance (January 1, 2003)		$ 25,000
Total change in cash during the year		60,000
Ending cash balance (December 31, 2003)		**$ 85,000**

*Computation:
Depreciation must be removed as it is a non-cash expense - a cash payment of $40,000 for depreciation does not occur. Thus, cash used for expenses equals: $400,000 - $40,000 = $360,000.

How This Chapter Relates to Other Chapters in This Book

This chapter consists of two cases. Each will require you to account for a corporation during a particular accounting period. You must use all the steps in the accounting cycle along with the four financial statements to complete each case.

Each case will allow you to practice the knowledge gained from Accounting for Corporations: Volume One. In addition, you will also rely upon the expertise gained in Volumes One, Two and Three of Fundamentals of Accounting. Should you encounter any difficulties, we encourage a review of the previously covered material.

Topics Covered in Chapter SIX

Case One
Drazel Cleaners Incorporated

Case Two
Temporary Solutions Limited

Case One

Drazel Cleaners Incorporated

John Drazel received a certificate of incorporation authorizing 50,000 no-par common shares for Drazel Cleaners Incorporated on January 1, 2004. The company was established to provide cleaning services to corporate offices located in the city. Currently, the company only has 2 employees, but it believes great opportunities exist for expansion. During the first month of operations the following activities took place:

Date	Activity
January 1	Issued 2,500 shares to John Drazel in exchange for $5 per share.
January 2	Paid the organization expenses amounting to $1,500.
January 3	Purchased cleaning supplies for $1,600 cash.
January 4	Purchased cleaning equipment for $8,000; half was paid in cash, the rest on credit that is due in thirty days.
January 8	Earned revenues of $4,200; $1,000 collected in cash, $3,200 on account.
January 15	Issued 500 shares to Mrs. Drazel in exchange for $5 per share, cash.
January 18	Purchased advertisement in local paper. Paid $200 cash.
January 22	Declared a dividend payment of $0.20 per share to all shareholders. Payment to be made at the end of this month.
January 30	Declared a dividend payment of $0.30 per share to all shareholders. Payment to be made on February 15, 2004
January 31	Paid the $0.20 dividend on 3,000 shares, declared January 22.
January 31	Incurred wage expenses of $700; paid cash $400, $300 payable in February.

The company has hired you as their bookkeeper. You are responsible for arranging and completing the accounting cycle for the month of January 2004. The shareholders would like all four financial statements prepared for this month.

Upon taking a physical count in the storeroom, you find there is $600 worth of cleaning supplies left. In addition, you estimate the cleaning equipment to have a life of 6 years with no salvage value. You will use straight-line depreciation. The company will pay income taxes on any income at a rate of 25%. Taxes will be paid every three months.

You may use the following spaces provided for your work. Once you have completed the financial statements, make one recommendation to the company.

Drazel Cleaners Incorporated - General Journal

First we analyze each transaction and record it in the General Journal.

Date	Debit $	Credit $
Explanation:		

Computation:

Date	Debit $	Credit $
Explanation:		

Date	Debit $	Credit $
Explanation:		

Date	Debit $	Credit $
Explanation:		

Date	Debit $	Credit $
Explanation:		

Date	Debit $	Credit $
Explanation:		

Computation:

Date	Debit $	Credit $
Explanation:		

Date	Debit $	Credit $
Explanation:		

Computation:

Date	Debit $	Credit $
Explanation:		

Computation:

Date	Debit $	Credit $
Explanation:		

Date		Debit $	Credit $
Explanation:			

Drazel Incorporated - General Ledger

Note: Include all postings, even closing entries in this space.

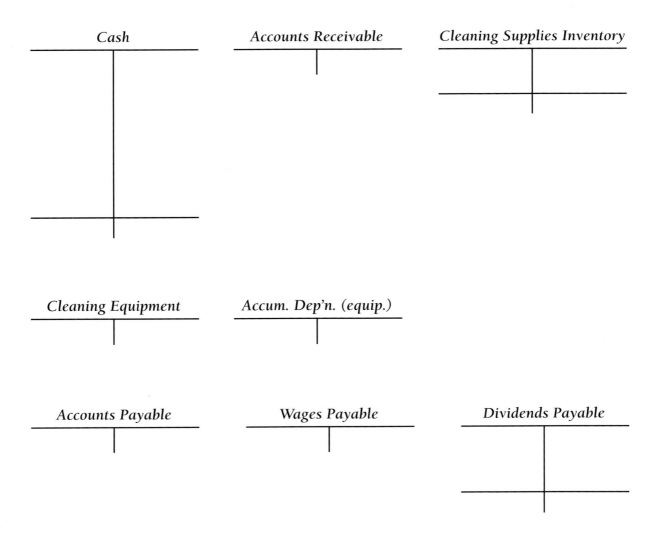

Cash

Accounts Receivable

Cleaning Supplies Inventory

Cleaning Equipment

Accum. Dep'n. (equip.)

Accounts Payable

Wages Payable

Dividends Payable

Income Taxes Payable

Share Capital

Retained Earnings

Cleaning Revenues

Wages Expense

Cleaning Supplies Expense

Advertising Expense

Depreciation Expense

Income Tax Expense

Organization Expense

Income Summary

Drazel Cleaners Incorporated
Trial Balance
As at _____

Account	Debit $	Credit $
TOTAL		

Drazel Cleaners Incorporated General Journal - Adjusting Entries

Date	Debit $	Credit $
Explanation:		

Computation:

Date	Debit $	Credit $
Explanation:		

Computation:

Date	Debit $	Credit $
Explanation:		

Computation:

Drazel Cleaners Incorporated
Adjusted Trial Balance
As at _____

Account	Debit $	Credit $
TOTAL		

Drazel Cleaners Incorporated
Income Statement

	$
Sales Revenue	
Expenses:	
Total Expenses	
Income before Taxes	
Income Tax Expense (25%)*	
Net Income	

Computation:

Drazel Cleaners Incorporated
Balance Sheet

Assets	**Liabilities**
	TOTAL (Liabilities)
	Shareholders' Equity
	TOTAL (Shareholders' Equity)
TOTAL (Assets)	TOTAL (Liabilities and Shareholders' Equity)

Drazel Cleaners Incorporated
Statement of Retained Earnings

Subtotal	

Note: This statement is somewhat complex. To assist you we have provided the titles of each entry.

Drazel Cleaners Incorporated
Statement of Cash Flows
For the month ended January 31, 2004

	Sub-totals	Totals
Cash Flows from Operations		
Cash received from customers	$	
Cash paid for organization expenses	$	
Cash paid for cleaning supplies		
Cash paid for advertising		
Cash paid for wages		
Cash increase (decrease) from operations		$
Cash Flows from Investing Activities		
Purchase of cleaning equipment	$	
Cash increase (decrease) from investing activities:		$
Cash Flows from Financing Activities		
Issuance of common shares	$	
Dividends paid		
Cash increase (decrease) from financing activities:		$
Increase (decrease) in cash during the month:		$7,700
Beginning cash balance (January 1, 2004)		0
Ending cash balance (January 31, 2004)		$7,700

One Recommendation:

_____

_____

_____

_____

_____

_____
_____
_____
_____
_____
_____
_____
_____
_____
_____
_____
_____
_____
_____

Drazel Cleaners Incorporated General Journal - Closing Entries

Date	Debit $	Credit $
Explanation:		

Date	Debit $	Credit $
Explanation:		

Date	Debit $	Credit $
Explanation:		

Date	Debit $	Credit $
Explanation:		

Date	Debit $	Credit $
Explanation:		

Date	Debit $	Credit $
Explanation:		

Date	Debit $	Credit $
Explanation:		

Date	Debit $	Credit $
Explanation:		

Along with the post-closing trial balance:

Drazel Cleaners Incorporated
Post-Closing Trial Balance
As at January 31, 2004

Account	Debit $	Credit $
TOTAL		

Solutions to Case One

Drazel Cleaners Incorporated - General Journal

First we analyze each transaction and record it in the General Journal.

Date January 1, 2004	Debit $	Credit $
Cash	12,500	
Share Capital		12,500
Explanation: To record the issue of 2,500 common shares at $5 each, for cash to John Drazel.		

Computation: *2,500 x $5 = $12,500*

Date January 2, 2004	Debit $	Credit $
Organization Expense	1,500	
Cash		1,500
Explanation: To record the payment for the organization expenses.		

Date January 3, 2004	Debit $	Credit $
Cleaning Supplies Inventory	1,600	
Cash		1,600
Explanation: To record purchase of cleaning supplies for cash.		

Date January 4, 2004	Debit $	Credit $
Cleaning Equipment	8,000	
Cash		4,000
Accounts Payable		4,000
Explanation: To record purchase of cleaning equipment, one-half cash, the remainder on credit.		

Date January 8, 2004	Debit $	Credit $
Cash	1,000	
Accounts Receivable	3,200	
Cleaning Revenues		4,200
Explanation: To record revenues of $4,200, including $3,200 on account.		

Date January 15, 2004	Debit $	Credit $
Cash	2,500	
Share Capital		2,500
Explanation: To record the issue of 500 shares at $5 each, for cash to Mrs. Drazel.		

Computation: 500 x $5 = $2,500

Date January 18, 2004	Debit $	Credit $
Advertising Expense	200	
Cash		200
Explanation: To record the advertising expense, paid with cash.		

Date January 22, 2004	Debit $	Credit $
Retained Earnings	600	
Dividends Payable		600
Explanation: To record the declaration of a $0.20 per share dividend on 3,000 shares, payable January 31.		

Computation: 3,000 x $0.20 = $600

Date January 30, 2004	Debit $	Credit $
Retained Earnings	900	
Dividends Payable		900
Explanation: To record the declaration of a $0.30 per share dividend on 3,000 shares, payable February 15.		

Computation: 3,000 x $0.30 = $900

Date January 31, 2004	Debit $	Credit $
Dividends Payable	600	
Cash		600
Explanation: To record payment of the $0.20 per share dividend.		

Date January 15, 2004	Debit $	Credit $
Wages Expense	700	
Wages Payable		300
Cash		400
Explanation: To record wages expenses; $400 for cash, the rest on account.		

Drazel Incorporated - General Ledger

Then we post the entries to the GL.   **Note:** Below we have included all postings, even closing entries.

Cash	
12,500	
	1,500
	1,600
	4,000
1,000	
2,500	200
	600
	400
7,700	

Accounts Receivable	
3,200	

Cleaning Supplies Inventory	
1,600	
	1,000
600	

Cleaning Equipment	
8,000	

Accum. Dep'n. (equip.)	
	111

Accounts Payable	
	4,000

Wages Payable	
	300

Dividends Payable	
	600
	900
600	
	900

Income Taxes Payable	
	172

Share Capital	
	12,500
	2,500
	15,000

Retained Earnings	
600	
900	
1,500	
	517
983	

Cleaning Revenues	
	4,200
4,200	
	0

Wages Expense	
700	
	700
0	

Cleaning Supplies Expense	
1,000	
	1,000
0	

Advertising Expense	
200	200
0	

Depreciation Expense	
111	111
0	

Income Tax Expense	
172	172
0	

Organization Expense	
1,500	1,500
0	

Income Summary	
	4,200
700	
1,000	
200	
111	
172	
1,500	
517	517
	0

Then, the trial balance:

Drazel Cleaners Incorporated
Trial Balance
As at January 31, 2004

Account	Debit $	Credit $
Cash	7,700	
Accounts Receivable	3,200	
Cleaning Supplies Inventory	1,600	
Cleaning Equipment	8,000	
Accounts Payable		4,000
Wages Payable		300
Dividends Payable		900
Share Capital		15,000
Retained Earnings	1,500	
Cleaning Revenues		4,200
Wages Expense	700	
Advertising Expense	200	
Organization Expense	1,500	
TOTAL	24,400	24,400

Notes

_____
_____
_____
_____
_____
_____
_____
_____
_____
_____
_____
_____

Followed by adjusting entries:

Drazel Cleaners Incorporated General Journal - Adjusting Entries

Date January 31, 2004	Debit $	Credit $
Cleaning Supplies Expense	1,000	
Cleaning Supplies Inventory		1,000
Explanation: To record cleaning supplies used during January 2004.		

Computation: $1,600 - $600 = $1,000 of cleaning supplies used during January 2004.

Date January 31, 2004	Debit $	Credit $
Depreciation Expense	111	
Accumulated Depreciation - Equipment		111
Explanation: To record depreciation expense for the month.		

Computation: ($8,000 - $0) ÷ 6 years = $1,333.33 per year.
$1,333.33 ÷ 12 months = $111.11 per month. We will round to $111.00.

Date January 18, 2004	Debit $	Credit $
Income Tax Expense	172	
Income Tax Payable		172
Explanation: To record income tax expense for January 2004, not yet paid.		

Computation:
Revenues and Expenses from the unadjusted trial balance total $4,200 and $2,400 respectively. The adjusting entry expenses total $1,111. Thus, total expenses equal $3,511. Pre-tax income is therefore the difference $689. Using the 25% tax rate: $689 x 25% = $172.25 in taxes owing. We will round this amount to $172.

And the adjusted trial balance:

Drazel Cleaners Incorporated
Adjusted Trial Balance
As at January 31, 2004

Account	Debit $	Credit $
Cash	7,700	
Accounts Receivable	3,200	
Cleaning Supplies Inventory	600	
Cleaning Equipment	8,000	
Accumulated Depreciation - Equipment		111
Accounts Payable		4,000
Wages Payable		300
Dividends Payable		900
Income Taxes Payable		172
Share Capital		15,000
Retained Earnings	1,500	
Cleaning Revenues		4,200
Wages Expense	700	
Advertising Expense	200	
Organization Expense	1,500	
Cleaning Supplies Expense	1,000	
Depreciation Expense	111	
Income Tax Expense	172	
TOTAL	24,683	24,683

Next prepare the financial statements:

Drazel Cleaners Incorporated
Income Statement
For the month ended January 31, 2004

Sales Revenue		$4,200
Expenses:		
Wages	$700	
Advertising	200	
Cleaning Supplies	1,000	
Depreciation	111	
Organization	1,500	
Total Expenses		3,511
Income before Taxes		689
Income Tax Expense (25%)*		172
Net Income		$ 517

Computation: *$689 x 25% = $172.

Notes

_____
_____
_____
_____
_____
_____
_____
_____
_____
_____
_____

Drazel Cleaners Incorporated
Balance Sheet
As at January 31, 2004

Assets		Liabilities	
Cash	$7,700	Accounts Payable	4,000
Account Receivable	3,200	Wages Payable	300
Cleaning Supplies Inventory	600	Dividends Payable	900
Cleaning Equipment	8,000	Income Taxes Payable	172
Less: Accumulated Depreciation	(111)	**TOTAL** (Liabilities)	**5,372**
		Shareholders' Equity	
		Share Capital: 50,000 no-par value common shares authorized; 3,000 shares issued.	15,000
		Retained Earnings (Deficit)*	(983)
		TOTAL (Shareholders' Equity)	**14,017**
TOTAL (Assets)	**$19,389**	**TOTAL** (Liabilities and Shareholders' Equity)	**$19,389**

* See Statement of Retained Earnings.

Notes

_____
_____
_____
_____
_____
_____
_____
_____
_____
_____
_____
_____

Drazel Cleaners Incorporated
Statement of Retained Earnings
For the month ended January 31, 2004

Retained Earnings balance, January 1, 2004	$0
Net Income for the month	<u>517</u>
Subtotal	517
Dividends Declared	<u>1,500</u>
Retained Earnings (Deficit) balance, January 31, 2004	**($983)**

Notes

_____
_____
_____
_____
_____
_____
_____
_____
_____
_____
_____
_____
_____
_____
_____
_____
_____
_____
_____
_____
_____

Drazel Cleaners Incorporated
Statement of Cash Flows
For the month ended January 31, 2004

	Sub-totals	Totals
Cash Flows from Operations		
Cash received from customers	$1,000	
Cash paid for organization expenses	($1,500)	
Cash paid for cleaning supplies	(1,600)	
Cash paid for advertising	(200)	
Cash paid for wages	(400)	
Cash increase (decrease) from operations		($2,700)
Cash Flows from Investing Activities		
Purchase of cleaning equipment	($4,000)	
Cash increase (decrease) from investing activities:		($4,000)
Cash Flows from Financing Activities		
Issuance of common shares	$15,000	
Dividends paid	(600)	
Cash increase (decrease) from financing activities:		$14,400
Increase (decrease) in cash during the month:		$7,700
Beginning cash balance (January 1, 2004)		0
Ending cash balance (January 31, 2004)		$7,700

One Recommendation:

The income statement shows only $517 was earned from operating the company during the month. Yet, the company declared $1,500 worth of dividends. Thus, the statement of retained earnings shows negative $983 has been "retained". There is a deficit. This is also reflected on the balance sheet. Investors would see the company is depleting its equity because dividends exceed income. They would find this undesirable. It would make selling more shares difficult, and would reduce the value of the issued shares.

In fact, we should be surprised that the board of directors approved the declaration for two reasons: 1) because it potentially harms the company 2) they made a decision before the financial reports were available - they did not have any information on which to base their decision. Perhaps the board members do not understand their duties.

The $600 payment has already been made, but the $900 dividend has not yet been paid. In addition, the company needs $4,000 to pay for the cleaning equipment, due in a few days. We recommend the declaration decision be reversed, if possible. As there are only two shareholders it should be easy to get them to agree, once they understand the implication of the dividend declaration. The board members should be seriously questioned as to why they approved it in the first place.

Last, we prepare and post the closing entries:

Drazel Cleaners Incorporated General Journal - Closing Entries

Date January 31, 2004	Debit $	Credit $
Cleaning Revenues	4,200	
Income Summary		4,200
Explanation: To close cleaning revenues to income summary		

Date January 31, 2004	Debit $	Credit $
Income Summary	700	
Wages Expense		700
Explanation: To close wages expense to income summary		

Date January 31, 2004	Debit $	Credit $
Income Summary	200	
Advertising Expense		200
Explanation: To close advertising expense to income summary		

Date January 31, 2004	Debit $	Credit $
Income Summary	1,500	
Organization Expense		1,500
Explanation: To close organization expense to income summary		

Date January 31, 2004	Debit $	Credit $
Income Summary	1,000	
Cleaning Supplies Expense		1,000
Explanation: To close cleaning supplies expense to income summary		

Date January 31, 2004	Debit $	Credit $
Income Summary	111	
Depreciation Expense		111
Explanation: To close depreciation expense to income summary		

Date January 31, 2004	Debit $	Credit $
Income Summary	172	
Income Tax Expense		172
Explanation: To close income tax expense to income summary		

Date January 31, 2004	Debit $	Credit $
Income Summary	517	
Retained Earnings		517
Explanation: To close income summary to retained earnings		

Along with the post-closing trial balance:

Drazel Cleaners Incorporated
Post-Closing Trial Balance
As at January 31, 2004

Account	Debit $	Credit $
Cash	7,700	
Accounts Receivable	3,200	
Cleaning Supplies Inventory	600	
Cleaning Equipment	8,000	
Accumulated Depreciation - Equipment		111
Accounts Payable		4,000
Wages Payable		300
Dividends Payable		900
Income Taxes Payable		172
Share Capital		15,000
Retained Earnings	983	
TOTAL	**20,483**	**20,483**

Case Two

Temporary Solutions Limited

Temporary Solutions Limited is a company that provides professional office support, for a fee. It provides secretarial, printing and mailing services to other businesses. The company received its certificate of incorporation at the beginning of 2004. Of the 100,000 $1 par-value authorized shares, 1,000 were issued to each of the five founding shareholders in exchange for a cash contribution of $8 per share. No other shares have been issued since that time.

This first year of operations seems to have been a success. Unfortunately, the bookkeeper left the firm just before the year-end. He had almost finished preparing the trial balance, as given below:

Temporary Solutions Limited
Trial Balance
As at December 31, 2004

Account	Debit $	Credit $
Cash	13,600	
Accounts Receivable	13,000	
Office Supplies	3,000	
Prepaid Insurance	2,400	
Office Equipment	15,000	
Land	20,000	
Accounts Payable		1,000
Bank Loan		20,000
Share Capital		?
Additional Paid-In Capital		?
Sales Revenue		46,550
Salaries Expense	30,750	
Office Rent Expense	5,100	
Utilities Expense	1,200	
Advertising Expense	900	
Organization Expense	2,600	
TOTAL	**107,550**	**?**

Computations:

The shareholders are anxious to understand the financial position and performance of the company. They would like to declare a dividend payment for themselves. They can see there is some cash in that account, but are unsure if they should declare a dividend and withdraw the cash. Your job is to advise them. However, you must first complete the trial balance (above) and then the accounting cycle. This includes preparing and posting the adjusting entries, preparing the financial statements and closing the books for the year ended December 31, 2004. Sufficient space has been provided for all entries.

Information pertaining to the adjusting entries is as follows:

- A physical count shows there is $2,000 of office supplies on hand.
- The insurance policy was for 2 years.
- The equipment is estimated to have a life of ten years, with a residual value of $5,000.
- Interest owing on the bank loan is for one year at a rate of 8% per year. The interest payment will be made in January 2005.
- Income taxes are determined at a rate of 20%, and will be paid in March 2005.

Once you have completed the financial statements you should clearly see why a cash dividend should not be declared.

Temporary Solutions Limited - General Ledger

Note: Use for all postings, including closing. We have provided all ledger headings.

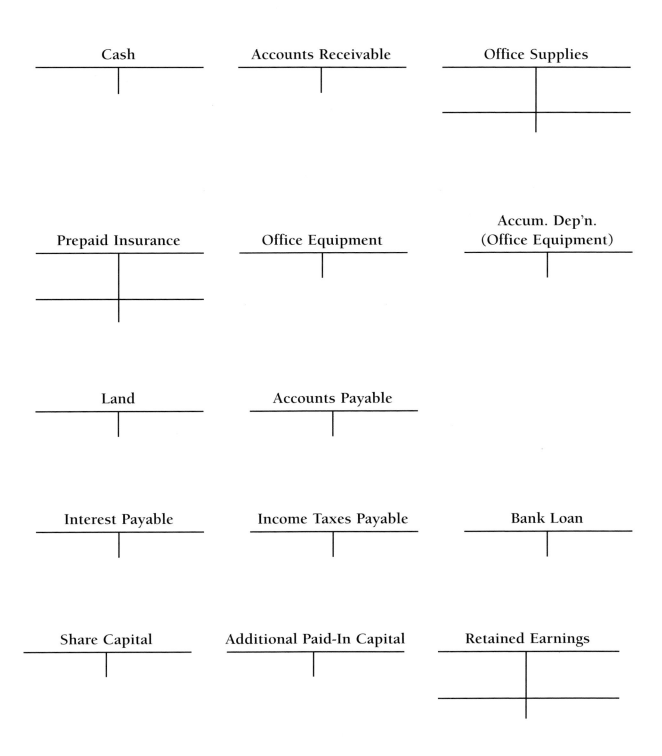

Cash   Accounts Receivable   Office Supplies

Prepaid Insurance   Office Equipment   Accum. Dep'n. (Office Equipment)

Land   Accounts Payable

Interest Payable   Income Taxes Payable   Bank Loan

Share Capital   Additional Paid-In Capital   Retained Earnings

Sales Revenue

Salaries Expense

Office Rent Expense

Advertising
Expense

Organization
Expense

Off. Supplies
Expense

Insurance
Expense

Depreciation Expense

Interest Expense

Income Tax Expense

Utilities Expense

Income Summary

Temporary Solutions Limited General Journal - Adjusting Entries

Date	Debit $	Credit $
Explanation:		

Computation:

Date	Debit $	Credit $
Explanation:		

Computation:

Date	Debit $	Credit $
Explanation:		

Computation:

Date	Debit $	Credit $
Explanation:		

Computation:

Date	Debit $	Credit $
Explanation:		

Computation:

Temporary Solutions Limited
Adjusted Trial Balance
As at December 31, 2004

Account	Debit $	Credit $
TOTAL		

Temporary Solutions Limited
Income Statement
For the year ended December 31, 2004

Sales Revenue	
Expenses:	
Income Tax Expense (20%)*	
Net Income	

Computation:

Notes

_____

_____

_____

_____

_____

_____

_____

_____

_____

_____

Temporary Solutions Limited
Balance Sheet
As at December 31, 2004

Assets	Liabilities
	TOTAL (Liabilities)
	Shareholders' Equity
	TOTAL (Shareholders' Equity)
TOTAL (Assets)	**TOTAL** (Liabilities and Shareholders' Equity)

Temporary Solutions Incorporated
Statement of Retained Earnings
For the year ended December 31, 2004

Retained Earnings balance, January 1, 2004	
Net Income for the year	
Retained Earnings balance, December 31, 2004	

This statement is quite complex. To assist you we have provided the titles of each entry. Follow these as a guide:

Temporary Solutions Incorporated
Statement of Cash Flows
For the year ended December 31, 2004

	Sub-totals	Totals
Cash Flows from Operations		
Cash received from customers	$ 1	
Cash paid for office supplies	$ 2	
Cash paid for insurance		
Cash paid for salaries		
Cash paid for rent		
Cash paid for utilities		
Cash paid for advertising		
Cash paid for organization expenses		
Cash increase (decrease) from operations		
Cash Flows from Investing Activities		
Purchase of office equipment	$	
Purchase of land		
Cash increase (decrease) from investing activities:		
Cash Flows from Financing Activities		
Issuance of common shares	$	
Bank loan		
Cash increase (decrease) from financing activities:		
Increase (decrease) in cash during the year:		$13,600
Beginning cash balance (January 1, 2004)		0
Ending cash balance (December 31, 2004)		$13,600

1. Sales Revenue minus increase in Accounts Receivable = Cash Received from Customers.

2. Office Supplies Purchased minus increase in Accounts Payable = Cash Paid for Office Supplies (assume that Accounts Payable relates to amounts owing to suppliers of office supplies only).

Temporary Solutions General Journal - Closing Entries

Date	Debit $	Credit $
Explanation:		

Date	Debit $	Credit $
Explanation:		

Date	Debit $	Credit $
Explanation:		

Date	Debit $	Credit $
Explanation:		

Date	Debit $	Credit $
Explanation:		

Date	Debit $	Credit $
Explanation:		

Date	Debit $	Credit $
Explanation:		

Date	Debit $	Credit $
Explanation:		

Date	Debit $	Credit $
Explanation:		

Date	Debit $	Credit $
Explanation:		

Date	Debit $	Credit $
Explanation:		

Date	Debit $	Credit $
Explanation:		

Temporary Solutions Limited
Post-Closing Trial Balance
As at December 31, 2004

Account	Debit $	Credit $
TOTAL		

Solutions to Case Two

First, complete the trial balance:

Temporary Solutions Limited
Trial Balance
As at December 31, 2004

Account	Debit $	Credit $
Cash	13,600	
Accounts Receivable	13,000	
Office Supplies	3,000	
Prepaid Insurance	2,400	
Office Equipment	15,000	
Land	20,000	
Accounts Payable		1,000
Bank Loan		20,000
Share Capital		5,000*
Additional Paid-In Capital		35,000*
Sales Revenue		46,550
Salaries Expense	30,750	
Office Rent Expense	5,100	
Utilities Expense	1,200	
Advertising Expense	900	
Organization Expense	2,600	
TOTAL	**107,550**	**107,550**

Computations:
1,000 shares x 5 shareholders = 5,000 shares issued.
*5,000 shares x $1 par = $5,000.
**5,000 x ($8 - $1) = $35,000.

Temporary Solutions Limited - General Ledger

Note: shows all postings, including closing.

Cash	
13,600	

Accounts Receivable	
13,000	

Office Supplies	
3,000	
	1,000
2,000	

Prepaid Insurance	
2,400	
	1,200
1,200	

Office Equipment	
15,000	

Accum. Dep'n. (Office Equipment)	
	1,000

Land	
20,000	

Accounts Payable	
	1,000

Interest Payable	
	1,600

Income Taxes Payable	
	240

Bank Loan	
	20,000

Share Capital	
	5,000

Additional Paid-In Capital	
	35,000

Retained Earnings	
	0
	960
	960

	Sales Revenue	
	46,550	
46,550		
	0	

	Salaries Expense	
30,750		
	30,750	
0		

	Office Rent Expense	
5,100		
	5,100	
0		

	Advertising Expense	
900	900	
0		

	Organization Expense	
2,600	2,600	
0		

	Off. Supplies Expense	
1,000	1,000	
0		

	Insurance Expense	
1,200	1,200	
0		

	Depreciation Expense	
1,000	1,000	
0		

	Interest Expense	
1,600	1,600	
0		

	Income Tax Expense	
240	240	
0		

	Utilities Expense	
1,200	1,200	
0		

Income Summary	
30,750	46,550
5,100	
1,200	
900	
2,600	
1,000	
1,200	
1,000	
1,600	
240	
	960
960	
	0

Next, prepare the adjusting entries:

Temporary Solutions Limited General Journal - Adjusting Entries

Date December 31, 2004	Debit $	Credit $
Office Supplies Expense	1,000	
Office Supplies		1,000
Explanation: To record office supplies used during the year 2004.		

Computation: $3,000 - $2,000 = $1,000 of office supplies used during 2004.

Date December 31, 2004	Debit $	Credit $
Insurance Expense	1,200	
Prepaid Insurance		1,200
Explanation: To record insurance expense for the year 2004.		

Computation: $2,400 ÷ 2 years = $1,000 per year.

Date December 31, 2004	Debit $	Credit $
Depreciation Expense	1,000	
Accumulated Depreciation - Equipment		1,000
Explanation: To record depreciation expense for the year 2004.		

Computation: ($15,000 - $5,000) ÷ 10 years = $1,000 per year.

Date December 31, 2004	Debit $	Credit $
Interest Expense	1,600	
Interest Payable		1,600
Explanation: To record interest expense for the year of 2004, not yet paid.		

Computation: $20,000 x 8% = $1,600 per year.

Date January 18, 2004	Debit $	Credit $
Income Tax Expense	240	
Income Taxes Payable		240
Explanation: To record income tax expense for the year 2004, not yet paid.		

Computation:

Revenues and Expenses from the trial balance total $46,550 and $40,550 respectively. The adjusting entry expenses total $4,800. Thus, total expenses equal $45,350. Pre-tax income is therefore the difference, namely $1,200. Using the 20% tax rate: $1,200 x 20% = $240 in taxes owing.

Notes

_____
_____
_____
_____
_____
_____
_____
_____
_____
_____
_____
_____
_____
_____
_____
_____
_____
_____
_____

Then, adjusted trial balance:

Temporary Solutions Limited
Adjusted Trial Balance
As at December 31, 2004

Account	Debit $	Credit $
Cash	13,600	
Accounts Receivable	13,000	
Office Supplies	2,000	
Prepaid Insurance	1,200	
Office Equipment	15,000	
Accumulated Depreciation - Equipment		1,000
Land	20,000	
Accounts Payable		1,000
Interest Payable		1,600
Income Taxes Payable		240
Bank Loan		20,000
Share Capital		5,000
Additional Paid-In Capital		35,000
Sales Revenue		46,550
Salaries Expense	30,750	
Office Rent Expense	5,100	
Utilities Expense	1,200	
Advertising Expense	900	
Organization Expense	2,600	
Office Supplies Expense	1,000	
Insurance Expense	1,200	
Depreciation Expense	1,000	
Interest Expense	1,600	
Income Tax Expense	240	
TOTAL	110,390	110,390

Next prepare the financial statements:

Temporary Solutions Limited
Income Statement
For the year ended December 31, 2004

Sales Revenue		**$46,550**
Expenses:		
Salaries	$30,750	
Office Rent	5,100	
Utilities	1,200	
Advertising	900	
Organization	2,600	
Office Supplies	1,000	
Insurance	1,200	
Depreciation	1,000	
Interest	<u>1,600</u>	
Total Expenses		<u>45,350</u>
Income before Taxes		1,200
Income Tax Expense (20%)*		<u>240</u>
Net Income		**$ 960**

Computation: **$1,200 x 20% = $240*

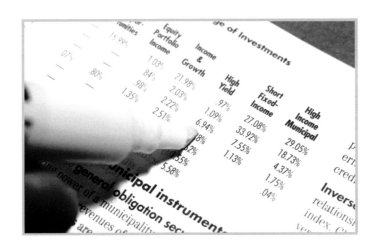

Temporary Solutions Limited
Balance Sheet
As at December 31, 2004

Assets		Liabilities	
Cash	$13,600	Accounts Payable	1,000
Account Receivable	13,000	Interest Payable	1,600
Office Supplies	2,000	Income Taxes Payable	240
Prepaid Insurance	1,200	Bank Loan	20,000
Office Equipment	15,000	**TOTAL** (Liabilities)	**22,840**
Less: Accumulated Depreciation	(1,000)		
Land	20,000	**Shareholders' Equity**	
		Share Capital: 10,000 $1 par-value common shares authorized; 5,000 shares issued.	5,000
		Additional paid-In Capital	35,000
		Retained Earnings (Deficit)*	960
		TOTAL (Shareholders' Equity)	**40,960**
TOTAL (Assets)	**$63,800**	**TOTAL** (Liabilities and Shareholders' Equity)	**$63,800**

Temporary Solutions Incorporated
Statement of Retained Earnings
For the year ended December 31, 2004

Retained Earnings balance, January 1, 2004	$0
Net Income for the year	960
Retained Earnings balance, December 31, 2004	**$960**

Temporary Solutions Incorporated
Statement of Cash Flows
For the year ended December 31, 2004

	Sub-totals	Totals
Cash Flows from Operations		
Cash received from customers	$33,550[1]	
Cash paid for office supplies	($ 2,000)[2]	
Cash paid for insurance	(2,400)	
Cash paid for salaries	(30,750)	
Cash paid for rent	(5,100)	
Cash paid for utilities	(1,200)	
Cash paid for advertising	(900)	
Cash paid for organization expenses	(2,600)	
Cash increase (decrease) from operations		(11,400)
Cash Flows from Investing Activities		
Purchase of office equipment	($15,000)	
Purchase of land	(20,000)	
Cash increase (decrease) from investing activities:		(35,000)
Cash Flows from Financing Activities		
Issuance of common shares	$40,000	
Bank loan	20,000	
Cash increase (decrease) from financing activities:		$60,000
Increase (decrease) in cash during the year:		$13,600
Beginning cash balance (January 1, 2004)		0
Ending cash balance (December 31, 2004)		$13,600

1. *Sales Revenue minus increase in Accounts Receivable = Cash Received from Customers.*

   $46,550 - $13,000 = $33,550.

2. *Office Supplies Purchased minus increase in Accounts Payable = Cash Paid for Office Supplies (assume that Accounts Payable relates to amounts owing to suppliers of office supplies only).*

$3,000 - $1,000 = $2,000.

The income statement and statement of retained earnings both show only $960 was earned from operating the company during the year. While a dividend could be declared for this amount, nothing would be retained for future investment. In addition, the statement of cash flows shows that operations used more cash than was brought in. Thus, a cash dividend should not be paid.

Last, we prepare and post the closing entries:

Temporary Solutions General Journal - Closing Entries

Date December 31, 2004	Debit $	Credit $
Sales Revenues	46,550	
Income Summary		46,550
Explanation: To close sales revenues to income summary.		

Date December 31, 2004	Debit $	Credit $
Income Summary	30,750	
Salaries Expense		30,750
Explanation: To close salaries expense to income summary.		

Date December 31, 2004	Debit $	Credit $
Income Summary	5,100	
Office Rent Expense		5,100
Explanation: To close office rent expense to income summary.		

Date December 31, 2004	Debit $	Credit $
Income Summary	1,200	
Utilities Expense		1,200
Explanation: To close utilities expense to income summary.		

Date December 31, 2004	Debit $	Credit $
Income Summary	900	
Advertising Expense		900
Explanation: To close advertising expense to income summary.		

Date December 31, 2004	Debit $	Credit $
Income Summary	2,600	
Organization Expense		2,600
Explanation: To close organization expense to income summary.		

Date December 31, 2004	Debit $	Credit $
Income Summary	1,000	
Office Supplies Expense		1,000
Explanation: To close office supplies expense to income summary.		

Date December 31, 2004	Debit $	Credit $
Income Summary	1,200	
Insurance Expense		1,200
Explanation: To close insurance expense to income summary.		

Date December 31, 2004	Debit $	Credit $
Income Summary	1,000	
Depreciation Expense		1,000
Explanation: To close depreciation expense to income summary.		

Date December 31, 2004	Debit $	Credit $
Income Summary	1,600	
Interest Expense		1,600
Explanation: To close interest expense to income summary.		

Date December 31, 2004	Debit $	Credit $
Income Summary	240	
Income Tax Expense		240
Explanation: To close income tax expense to income summary.		

Date December 31, 2004	Debit $	Credit $
Income Summary	960	
Retained Earnings		960
Explanation: To close income summary to retained earnings.		

Along with the post-closing trial balance:

Temporary Solutions Limited
Post-Closing Trial Balance
As at December 31, 2004

Account	Debit $	Credit $
Cash	13,600	
Accounts Receivable	13,000	
Office Supplies	2,000	
Prepaid Insurance	1,200	
Office Equipment	15,000	
Accumulated Depreciation - Equipment		1,000
Land	20,000	
Accounts Payable		1,000
Interest Payable		1,600
Income Taxes Payable		240
Bank Loan		20,000
Share Capital		5,000
Additional Paid-In Capital		35,000
Retained Earnings		960
TOTAL	64,800	64,800

Notes

Notes

Notes

Notes

Notes

Notes